"Powerful! Packed with actionable practices and relevant research, Gregg Brown's compelling new book provides the tools you need to start making a difference today!"

MARSHALL GOLDSMITH, Thinkers50 #1 executive coach and _New York Times_–bestselling author of _What Got You Here Won't Get You There_

"Want to freshen up how you show up? Gregg Brown has so many teachables from his gritty and graceful work with leaders. _Spark Action_ is the practical wisdom that can only come from someone who's helped a lot of people shift into higher gear—for _real_."

DANIELLE LAPORTE, creator of The Desire Map and The Heart Centered Leadership Program

"Filled with actionable tools and engaging stories, _Spark Action_ inspires positive change in you and in the people you lead. Spark your leadership toolkit, and make change that matters. Read this book now!"

ADAM KREEK, executive business coach, Olympic gold medalist, and author of _The Responsibility Ethic_

"Gregg Brown is a natural storyteller, and through his relatable examples, relevant research, and practical advice, _Spark Action_ will show you how to be the kind of change-maker that helps people excel."

MARK TEWKSBURY, CC, MSM, Olympic gold medalist, leader, advocate

"Brilliant writer and speaker Gregg Brown finally answers the deep calling we all feel inside: how we can enact real and lasting change in the world. In this witty, fun, and thoughtful book, Gregg teaches you exactly that and so much more."

ROBYN YOUKILIS, wellness expert and author of *Go With Your Gut* and *Thin from Within*

"*Spark Action* is urgent yet compassionate, bold yet pragmatic, and comprehensive yet concise. Whether you're trying to overcome self-doubt, galvanize colleagues and customers, or change the world, Gregg Brown's latest book is a fire-starter for those eager to spark their ideas into action."

HAMZA KHAN, future of work expert and author of *Leadership, Reinvented*

"The essential road map for inspiring others to make the change you need. A practical springboard for making immediate impact that lasts."

PHIL BUCKLEY, author of *Change on the Run* and *Change with Confidence*

"An original spark, indeed a righteous troublemaker, Gregg Brown puts forth a masterclass book where his wonderful wisdom and tips for action will spawn the kind of good change habits you never knew you needed."

DAN PONTEFRACT, author of *Work-Life Bloom*

"*Spark Action* will help future-proof you and your business."

PETER SHEAHAN, C-suite advisor

SPARK ACTION

GREGG BROWN

How to Lead Change That Matters

SPARK
ACTION

Cataloguing in publication information is
available from Library and Archives Canada.
ISBN 978-1-77458-322-7 (paperback)
ISBN 978-1-77458-323-4 (ebook)

Page Two
pagetwo.com

Edited by James Harbeck
Copyedited by Steph VanderMeulen
Proofread by Alison Strobel
Cover and interior design by Cameron McKague
Printed and bound in Canada by Friesens
Distributed in Canada by Raincoast Books
Distributed in the US and internationally by Macmillan

23 24 25 26 27   5 4 3 2 1

sparkactionbook.com

This book is dedicated to you.
The one who wants to lead change that matters.

Contents

INTRODUCTION
My Story

"I am my best work—a series of road maps, reports, recipes, doodles, and prayers from the front lines."

AUDRE LORDE, poet

I WAS TWENTY-SIX YEARS OLD and had just had my contract at a ski resort canceled after one season—which means I was fired.

I was happy about that. The whole thing wasn't a fit. I'd left a structured role, with policies, processes, and a good team, for a very open and different environment. The job—in a remote mountain resort, isolated from my friends and family—was just not for me. So I was relieved. But my work self-esteem took a hit.

I loaded up my car, a big gas-guzzling Chrysler Cordoba, drove back to Vancouver, and camped out in a spare bedroom on a friend's farm.

So what was I going to do with my life? I wasn't in a rush to do anything—I wanted my next job to be a good one. I had bounced around from one job to another every few years, each time growing a little, yet I felt there was something bigger on the planet I was meant to do. But what?

As I was looking through books on a shelf, one popped out at me. I remember it had an orange cover. It was one of those motivational books with religious overtones, but the important thing was that it included stories of people who had been in situations similar to mine.

I started reading. One line stood out for me, something to the effect of "anything is possible." While that sounds trite to me today, at the time, I had felt very limited by my options. The stories inspired me to think differently. After all, if other people could turn their lives around, why couldn't I?

And just like that, a magic wand . . . did not suddenly appear overnight. That's not my story! However, what did happen is this.

One morning while reading a newspaper, I came across an article about an inmate in a Canadian prison being denied access to health care—I don't even remember what the reasons were.

My back went up. "This is Canada!" I thought. "Everyone can access health care here, regardless of background or who you are." And there I was, this naive little white bread kid who grew up in a lower-middle-class neighborhood, all fired up about this man's fate.

I hadn't met anyone who had been to jail—that I knew of, anyway. I had no experience with the criminal justice system. Yet the story triggered something in me. I did not question it. I phoned the person who wrote the article and said, "I need to get involved."

That one call brought me here today.

The Journey

There are two ways to create change that matters. One is as an activist—getting media attention, protesting, putting pressure on causes or organizations from the outside. The other is as an educator or advocate. While activism is very much needed, I'm much more personally comfortable with and interested in how to get people engaged in my ideas.

Ultimately, just like you, I want people to take action on what I'm saying. What's the point otherwise?

While many of you may not work inside a jail, or with people living on the street, or teach sexual health to Catholic nuns (see chapter 10), these diverse early experiences shaped my insights and processes on how to create messages so that people hear you and your points, so you can spark action in others—ultimately, so you can lead and create change that matters. Today, I apply this knowledge in my work with leaders, teams, and organizations on leading change, navigating the future, and other topics related to change and leadership development, and in my volunteer work when I'm mentoring and coaching young entrepreneurs. Whether one-on-one or in a small group of twenty or a large group of a thousand, I want to spark action in someone to do something with what I say.

That's the whole reason for this book: to help you engage others in your ideas so they take action. Any of these circumstances could describe you:

- You are a leader who has an inspiring vision you want your team to engage in—why won't they get on board?

- You are someone in an organization who has to get others to take action on your project, but people see it as another make-work project.

- You are an entrepreneur who has a valuable service to share with the world... why won't people buy it?

- You are passionate about a cause.

- You have an idea you think is important and you want to get it out there.

- You are unsure about why people don't take action on your ideas.

The ideas and strategies contained in this book will help you. They've worked for me and I've seen them work for thousands of people in a variety of circumstances. I know that if I can do this and they can do this, then so can you.

Creating the Space for Change

Too often we've been told to sell, sell, sell to people and convince them that our ideas are right. But I've seen from experience that people shut down when we do that. And even if we convince them we're right and they agree with our idea, it does not mean they're going to take action on it.

We can't make people change. It's important we let go of the mindset that we can swoop in and save everybody and make people do things. We can't, and that's not our job. What we can do is create an environment for change, where our audience can hear our message, be receptive to it, feel safe enough to ask questions and discuss issues, and then want to take action.

Often, I was told, the biggest difference I made to the guys in jail wasn't just with the workshops I led; it was also in the way I treated them, shaking their hands and calling them by their first names. Among other things, this created an opportunity for them to hear me. Finding those places where we can connect as humans is critical. We must find a way to relate. There are many similar experiences people share. Finding them is key.

Some years back, a picture of an obese woman who had fallen off her scooter trying to reach an item on a grocery shelf went viral on social media. In the post's comments, people laughed and many said hurtful things. While I did not comment, I did laugh when I first saw the picture. And then I forgot about it—until I opened up a popular news site and saw an article on this woman.

Incredibly, she had decided to hit back at her online trolls. She had scrolled through the cruel comments directed at her and decided to describe the impact that the humiliating experience had on her. What people thought they were seeing in this photo was a large woman tipped out of her scooter because she was too lazy to get out of the cart to grab a case of soda. As it turns out, she has a condition known as spondylolisthesis; its most common symptom is painful, weak legs. She can't stand or walk for long periods of time. She was simply grocery shopping, and she shamed her trolls for thinking that her obesity was a result of laziness.

Lesson learned.

But there was more. This story ignited a memory of me at ten years old, trick-or-treating as a cowboy for Halloween. Because I had nice, longish hair, blue eyes, and red lips, people assumed I was a girl and at countless houses said something like, "Oh, you're such a beautiful little cowgirl." I can look back and laugh at it now—I *was* rather pretty with nice hair (and I have *no* hair on my head now)—but at the time, I felt hurt. Why couldn't people see I was a cowboy?!

I realized I could relate to the woman's experience of humiliation. Then I knew I had created change within myself.

That's where all good change begins, right?

Breaking Barriers and Finding Your Cause

So the outcome of all my varied career experiences is that I have learned how people tick. And if I have something important to share with others, whether it's an individual or an organization, how can I say it in a way that allows people to hear me and relate?

It's not about shouting from the rooftops or striding across the stage or room with enthusiasm. Sometimes when I'm speaking, I have to be very conscious of not letting my passion override my message. Don't get me wrong:

passion is great in delivery, but you also need to channel that energy into asking the right questions and framing things in a way that makes people able and willing to take action on what you want them to do. I've worked with people on the street and in prison teaching life skills, and I've talked about sexual health and preventing STIs. I've taught leadership development in a corporate setting and worked with entrepreneurs to help them shift and grow their entrepreneurial mindset. The common thread in all of these circumstances is this: each time, I had to figure out what people needed to know about my topic and how I could help them create the space where they could learn. Getting people to hear you and be on board is about breaking through their barriers and perceptions—just like the woman who tipped over her motorized scooter did for me.

There are many important areas of interest in which people could learn so much. You can't cover them all. You can't cover even more than a few. You're just one person! You need to figure out what it is you want to do and where you can create the biggest change. The trick to that is to really pay attention to where your interest and energy go. By that, I mean asking questions like these:

- What makes me feel more open or more closed?
- Does this make me excited or not?
- Do I feel energized when I think about this?
- Would I do this if I wasn't paid?

For me, it was the article about the prisoner—just one of many—who spoke out about being denied access to health care that lit a fire inside. You may have a moment

of realization like that. But you might not. You might figure it out just by following your energy.

Speaking Your Truth

We've all been in that meeting. The one where we present what we think is a good idea and it's shot down
almost as soon as we say it: "Oh, that won't work. We
tried it before at my previous workplace, and it was a
total failure."

What happens next? We retreat into ourselves and
clam up, in fear of saying the wrong thing or presenting
another "unworkable" idea. Why be insulted and humil-
iated and accomplish nothing?

These days, we talk a lot about being our authentic
selves. Whether it's at home or work, we want to be who
we really are, to speak our truths, to live honestly and as
simply and straightforwardly as possible, and not have
to suffer quietly inside by withholding from others the
unique parts of ourselves. But sharing these truths, however liberating, can also be terrifying. It's hard to unlearn
the societal and corporate "stuff" we've amassed over our
lifetimes. After experiencing admonishment or shame for
speaking our truths, we often decide it's safer to close
ourselves to the world and open up to only those in our
closest circles.

The result is that we disconnect from others, leaving them to decide for themselves who we are, what we
stand for, and what our business and life missions are
about. We give them all the power to form their own

conclusions and act on their perspectives of us, whether or not they are accurate—and then we blame them for their misperceptions.

In business, we don't really tell people exactly what we offer, so they move on to the next option because they don't understand. Or we put up barriers, create conflict, and fail to negotiate for what we truly want. Sometimes, we react inappropriately.

What's the cost of not getting our voice out? For one thing, it creates a false sense of security. It can also lead to financial insecurity, especially if it comes with an inability to negotiate. Respect and dignity may be lost, as people perceive us as silent followers rather than powerful and inspiring leaders. But one of the most important losses is the ability to create a sense of psychological safety within our team—one based on commitment, engagement, and trust.

Over the years, I've learned that roughly 10 percent of people are probably not going to like me or you for whatever reason—you have too much hair or not enough, you're too tall, too short, too thin, too heavy, you speak too fast or too slow. The list goes on. It's inevitable, so it's not meaningful.

Your education and experiences as you age can obviously give you a bit of confidence and ability—my master's degree gave me confidence in my ability to talk about certain topics, and years of evaluations and speaking gave me more. Skill development and practice can also give you the confidence to engage others in your ideas.

Sometimes we are afraid to bring up our ideas because we think they're not good. The truth is, nobody brings a fully developed idea to a meeting. If we spend time exploring the ideas and allowing them to collide, new, innovative ideas will come to light. Creating lasting change begins with ideas and compelling stories. The best CEOs, corporate leaders, entrepreneurs, managers— any human being who wants to engage others in their ideas—connect to others with their heads *and* hearts. They listen empathically, internalizing what is being shared, and then synthesize their response with stories that best connect and illustrate potential solutions that result in a win-win situation. They create a link to their experience to reframe and communicate in a way that is universal rather than limited. This makes others feel empowered. Valued. But mostly, *heard*. When people feel heard, they are more likely to take action.

Find what energizes you. Speak your truth about it. I will keep speaking mine. We can't change the whole world, but we can work together to make a small or large difference in other people's lives. I believe that's worth doing. It's worth the risk. And you believe that too, or you wouldn't be here.

This book is about how to spark action and engage others in your ideas; how to speak (and listen) authentically, honestly, and powerfully; and how to develop leadership competencies so you can use your voice to create and lead change that truly matters in your life, your community, your organization, and the world.

Are you ready to get your voice out there so others can engage in your ideas to take action? It all starts with *you*! Yes, the wonderful part of you that wants to change the world.

Let's get started, shall we?

1

A PhD in Yourself

"There is a vitality, a life force, a quickening that is translated through you into action, and because there is only one of you in all time, this expression is unique. And if you block it, it will never exist through any other medium and be lost. The world will not have it."

MARTHA GRAHAM, dancer and choreographer,
to Agnes de Mille

YOU'RE HERE FOR A REASON.

I mean that two ways. First, you're here on this planet for a reason. We all are. When we find and follow our purpose, we create opportunities for growth and change. When we don't, we're not operating to our fullest potential—and in order to create and lead change, you need to bring everything you've got to the party.

Second, you're here reading this book for a reason. You need to connect and engage with people, which is not as easy as it looks on paper. If it were easier, you wouldn't be reading this book.

Whether you're a coach who wants to get your voice out there in the digital world, or a change leader in an organization, or a consultant trying to figure out your business direction, or a facilitator wanting to engage others in a diversity and inclusion workshop, or a speaker who gives talks on potentially tricky topics like drug addiction, you need to learn how to frame your stories in a way that compels people to hear you and make their own connections. You need to share your "original medicine" (an Indigenous concept) with people so that it combines with theirs in an elixir of powerful new truths—the kind that conjures action and makes change happen.

To do this, you need to use your voice to create the dialogue that facilitates change. *You* don't make the change happen. You can't make people change. You can only guide others to want the change to happen, and then work together to make it so. The real change happens in their minds first, or collectively within the group, and then the external change processes happen.

Before you can create change, though, you need to know who is leading that change. You need to know what your purpose is, what motivates you, and how not to get in your own way. You need to get a PhD in yourself.

Getting Expert Info on Yourself

The first thing in learning about yourself is to learn how others see you. It's not easy to ask, but you can start by interviewing people who know you well and who have seen you at your best and worst. They know you in ways that may be hard to witness for yourself unless you record and review your own performance (spoiler alert: most people don't have the stomach for that kind of self-reflection). I suggest you ask yourself and the people around you the following kinds of questions.

About you:

• Where do I thrive?

• Where do I shine?

- Why are we friends?

- What do you enjoy about me?

  About you as a communicator:

- What one thing could I do differently to make my voice heard?

- What ticks you off about me when we communicate?

- What language do I use that may be problematic?

- What stories could I tell from other people's perspectives for greater impact and connection?

As a speaker who has been onstage as well as teaching workshops for years, I get evaluation forms that give me feedback, so I have a good picture of my strengths and challenges. Other people's perspectives offer incredibly valuable information on which you can build a solid foundation so you can learn to connect with others on a heart level in addition to the informational level. By seeing what they see in you, you learn what you can use to connect with them. A big part of that comes from the empathic ability to see and understand things from others' perspectives.

You also need to observe—and be honest about—what tasks you're good at and when. Managing your energy is important in learning about yourself and how you work best. Different types of work take different types of energy. Administration takes extra energy for me, so I schedule it early in the morning, after preparing for it the day before. My more creative work also happens in the morning. I can disengage easily from really intense tasks later in the day, and my energy by the end of the day is usually drawn to preparing for the following day. I know not everyone has the ability to schedule tasks when they want, but if you have some control over your work schedule, determine what times are best for you to do certain types of work.

Motivation also comes into play when you want to spark action in others. Challenges will arise and you'll need to be able to get through them. You have to find a way to stay motivated as you lead others down the path of change.

You can ask yourself questions like:

- What motivates me in my work?

- Why do I want to take this on?

- What work am I most proud of and why?

- If I keep doing this work, what will be the outcome?

- What do I need to get out of this to stay engaged and motivated?

Getting Out of Your Own Way

The next thing to become good at is getting out of your own way. You need to learn how to not grind your wheels in the "analysis paralysis" that keeps you from moving forward.

Being unsure about yourself or about how to proceed is not an excuse to stop working on your goal. Even without all the information, you can explore ideas and take action.

As part of my volunteer work, I mentor and coach young entrepreneurs. I was coaching a young entrepreneur whom I'll call Mark. Mark was outlining for me approximately thirty items he was working on. As he went on and on, I gently interrupted him, saying, "You need to prioritize. Pick one of these items and start working the crap out of it."

The one thing Mark really wanted to do was create a podcast. I asked why he hadn't started. His response: "Yeah, I was thinking about it. But then I realized, probably no one's going to listen." He had already talked himself out of doing it before we'd even talked about it.

I suggested that we could in fact *explore* the idea and talk about the factors involved in getting a podcast going without him committing to it just yet. He didn't actually have to start it; we'd just get some ideas out about the podcast, such as a relevant topic that excited him, when he would record the podcast episodes, whom he would interview, where he would post, whom he would advertise it to. Within one hour of just exploring the idea, he had come up with a plan that excited him and sparked him to take action.

Mark thanked me for the great ideas. I said, "All I did was create the space and time for you to explore your idea instead of shutting it down. You allowed your ideas to collide and—*bam!*—you created a plan for a podcast in under an hour."

Your self-imposed limitations about what you can or cannot do are your greatest barrier to change and to getting others engaged in your ideas. So don't talk yourself out of your ideas before you've even started!

You are much more ready to lead change than you think you are. And you can do much more than you think you can.

"Who Am I to Talk About This?" (a.k.a. Imposter Syndrome)

One of the biggest and most common self-imposed limitations is the belief that you're not good enough to be doing what you're doing. This is known as "imposter syndrome." According to a 2020 study on imposter syndrome by Dena M. Bravata and her colleagues, 82 percent of the population face feelings of being an imposter at some point during their lives. My belief is that the other 18 percent experience it but don't realize it. I've worked and spoken with thousands of people for the past thirty or so years, and, to be honest, I don't know anyone who hasn't experienced it, regardless of age, education, experience, or even the awards they've received.

Additionally, people who work or live outside of the so-called mainstream nine-to-five environment, such as entrepreneurs, coaches, and self-employed consultants, are particularly prone to experiencing this because so many things, such as credit scores, bank loans, mortgages, and extended health-care benefits, are financially geared to the traditionally employed worker. As someone who has their own business, I see that the system has generally not been set up to align with the work self-employed entrepreneurs do. That can bring up questions for us such as, "Should I be doing this? Maybe I should have a nine-to-five job. How am I going to justify my work and income to get a mortgage?" Many of us entrepreneurs are on our own and don't have outside input, so we can get caught up in our heads, questioning things over and over. The sense of isolation and not having the overall systems aligned with self-employed individuals can also create imposter syndrome: "Who am I to be doing this?"

And the bigger our goals, the bigger our sense of being an imposter. When we want to spark action and create change that matters, we can often be faced with the questions, "Who am I to create this change?" and "Why should anyone listen to me?" We may be passionate about our topic but feel we don't have the qualifications or experience to start creating this change. People who have already accomplished much may chalk up their successes to sheer luck.

Minimizing your successes by not owning them is not helpful to your cause. You don't want to be boastful, yet you need to own what you are good at and why and be able to articulate it in a way that gives people confidence in you, even when you don't have confidence in yourself. Accomplishing things is harder if you're undermining or downgrading the person who is accomplishing them— even (or especially) when that person is yourself.

Regardless of how or why you may feel like an imposter, this syndrome is all about the negative stories you tell yourself that may be holding you back from leading and creating change that matters. It's easy to get stuck in what I call "inner trash talk." But stories matter, as we'll see again and again in this book, and the first stories that matter are the ones you tell yourself *about* yourself.

Here are a few ways I've found helpful to rewrite these stories, so you can step up to what you are being called to do. I've used them myself and with many others. Just pick one and try it!

- Create a "community of understanding" or a "board of directors" for your idea. Find mentors who can guide you. Seek out others who think like you and will support you and your ideas. You can even follow the examples of people you've never met but admire: "How would Maya Angelou respond?"

- Don't wait till things are perfect. Just start! Create a plan, then be flexible in how it unfolds. You may find in six months that you're going in a completely different direction, which is fine as long as it's supporting the overall goal and is something you really want to do.

- Build trust by sharing with others what you are not good at and what you could use help with. You can't do everything, and neither can anyone else! When you focus on working in your "zone"—in other words, on your strengths—the magic starts to happen.

- If something goes wrong, don't get stuck in the self-blame game. Ask, "What can I learn from this?"

- Talk about imposter syndrome with people. When you do, you'll find that other people experience it as well!

We all do, regardless of education, background, or experience. I've met seventy-five-year-olds with it and twenty-year-olds with it.

- Remember, worries are just made-up negative stories. So ground them in fact by asking, "What's the likelihood of this happening?" and "If it does happen, what will the impact be?" Research shows we tend to overestimate risk and make it worse when we don't quantify it or put some grading around it, or find other data points related to the risk.

- Write the change you want to cause on your bathroom mirror with an erasable marker. Anything you have around that reminds you of where you want to go can help knock you out of imposter syndrome thinking. You may feel silly writing your goal on a mirror—but guess what, that's just a negative story too! Reminders work. I know. I have things written on mirrors, and I have a guiding principle written on the window above my desk that I see every day. I don't care if people think it's silly—it works!

Remember this quote: "There's nothing enlightened about shrinking so that other people won't feel insecure around you." So true! This quote is often attributed to Nelson Mandela, but Marianne Williamson is the original author. She continues, "As we let our own light shine, we unconsciously give other people permission to do the same."

Can I get an "Amen!" to that?

TALKING POINTS

- Learn how others see you—ask them!

- Become aware of self-imposed limitations.

- Overcome imposter syndrome by rewriting the stories you tell yourself about yourself. You are readier to lead change than you think you are.

- Put up signposts, such as writing on your mirror, to knock you out of negative thinking.

2

Your Brain: Your Enemy, Your Friend

"Knowing yourself is the beginning of all wisdom."
ARISTOTLE

NOW IT'S TIME to dig even deeper. What we've looked at so far is governed by your mindset, which obviously is going on inside your head—meaning, of course, your brain.

One of the key things about human beings: when we set a goal in place, our subconscious mind, along with our mindset, figures out how to get there. "Mindset" isn't some woo-woo term; it's a collection of neurons in our prefrontal cortex where our executive functioning resides (for more about this, read "This Is Your Brain in Meltdown" in the April 2012 issue of *Scientific American*). These neurons in our prefrontal cortex determine how we're going to view problems and solve them, as well as how we make decisions throughout the day. And we can program these neurons to create new neural pathways with the words we use!

For example, if you get up in the morning and it's raining outside and your response is, "Oh, it's a lousy day out there," your brain is going to program you to notice "lousy" things throughout your day, and your mindset won't be primed to be as efficient as it can be.

If instead you just say, "It's a wet day out there," the neutral language keeps negative emotion from getting into your mindset and clouding your judgment. This isn't putting a positive spin on a bad situation. It's simply being objective.

Managing your mindset through the words you choose doesn't mean bad things won't happen, but it does mean that you'll be in a better frame of mind to handle them when they do happen. It also means that you're helping manage other people's mindsets. When you consciously or unconsciously use negative emotional language instead of objective language to describe things, it affects your hearers' mindsets—and can even cause people to disengage from hearing you.

Three Brains

The brain is a vastly complex thing, with far more layers and parts than we could discuss here. So, to simplify, there are three parts—three different brains within our brains—that matter for us on this topic:

- **Cognitive:** where all the reasoning and executive skills take place

- **Limbic:** the part that tries to protect you from danger

- **Amygdala:** the reptilian or reactive area that detects threats

If your mind is a bus, your cognitive brain sits at the front—it's what you want driving the bus most of the time. Typically, it's where your IQ resides as well as your executive functioning, mindset, reasoning, and ability to think things through clearly, plan for the future, and be proactive.

Your limbic system is your reactive brain—your affective, emotional brain—and it works 10,000 times faster than your cognitive brain. It's designed differently. The cognitive brain plans your future; the limbic brain protects the here and the now. It's designed to stop you from doing things that might be dangerous and to respond quickly to situations you may determine are threatening.

The amygdala is what some people call the reptilian brain. It's the scanner that, at the basest level, produces the fight-or-flight response—what Daniel Goleman calls the "amygdala hijack" in his book *Emotional Intelligence*.

Imagine you're mowing the lawn in front of your house. You're mowing in nice straight lines, using your cognitive brain so you cover the whole lawn and also don't cut off your toes. Suddenly, you see a kid playing in the middle of the street with cars coming. You don't use your cognitive brain at this point to determine the speed or velocity of that car. No, the amygdala leaps into action: it's detected a threat so it sends cortisol and adrenaline coursing through your body. Your heart rate and blood pressure increase. Your kidneys release glucose, a sugar that gives you the energy to combat the stressor. This is the best part: your brain gets flooded with cortisol and other chemicals. And guess what? You actually lose working memory, and your good old cognitive brain that was driving the bus isn't driving the bus anymore. Your limbic system is now the captain. Within seconds, you've let go of your lawnmower. You've run out into the middle of the street and pulled the kid out of the path of the car. And you're back at your lawnmower before you even know it.

Now let's say instead that you're in a meeting. You're talking through a problem with the group, using your cognitive brain. You suggest a plan of action, and someone says, "No way—I've been here eleven years and I know that'll never work." You shut down—your reptilian brain processes this as a threat. It's not life-threatening (probably), and maybe consciously you wouldn't say it's a threat, but your limbic system has kicked in and you're now experiencing the conversation differently from how you were a minute ago. Your brain is flooded with cortisol, and that will take a while to clear.

When someone starts sharing new information, it is natural for others to detect that new information as contrary to what they perceive as the truth, or different from what they know based on their past experience. This completely normal response is how we question and process new details to determine their truth and validity. But it is also where many audiences shut down, so it's important to know how to position your idea in a way that circumnavigates this natural tendency, so you can inspire action rather than doubt.

To engage others in your ideas and lead change that matters to you, you want to be careful not to activate people's reptilian brains while you are talking with them, just as you want to be careful to keep your own reptilian brain from activating so you can hear what people are saying and plan for the future.

This is often easier said than done! An important part of this is what you decide to focus on.

Where the Focus Goes

There's one more part of your brain you should know about: your reticular activating system (RAS). Located at the top of your brain stem, the RAS is a collection of neurons that regulates many functions in your body. It also tells you what to pay attention to. You could describe it as your attention filter.

When you teach a kid how to ride a bike, you tell them to look at where they want to go. If there's a path with a rock beside it, you tell them to focus on the path, not the rock, otherwise, their body will steer them toward the rock and they'll hit it.

But the RAS has a broader influence than that. You know when you buy a new car and it suddenly seems as if there are tons of other people also driving the same car? Or if you're pregnant, you start seeing other pregnant women everywhere? It's not that there are actually more pregnant women, or that everyone has the same new car as yours. What has happened is that you've unconsciously told your brain what to pay attention to, and now subconsciously your brain is looking for information that makes it happen. You're programming attention.

If I asked you to draw the home screen of your mobile phone—without looking at it—with all the apps labeled and in the right place, I guarantee you couldn't do it. Yet you look at your home screen probably a hundred times a day! The information is right in front of you, but you don't consciously retain it because other things have your attention. But if I told you in the next hour to notice where the apps are every time you open your mobile, you could probably draw the home screen after a while. Why? Because I've directed your attention to it.

When you have a goal and an end result in mind (whether positive or negative), your RAS will find evidence and examples to support it. When you're setting a goal, because you've told your brain it's important, your brain will start noticing the things that are going to help get you there. If you don't have goals, your brain won't know where to look.

This is why the words you use matter. If you keep saying, "I can't figure this out," that will become your focus and you will get more of "I can't figure this out." Instead, focus your language on the future and say, "I am going to figure this out." Then you are putting a goal in place, and your brain will be activated to notice ways to figure it out. Next time you're stuck trying to solve something and your inner voice is saying, "I don't know what to do," catch your language and say instead, "I'm going to figure this out." I guarantee ideas will start to flow in three minutes! I know this from my own experience and the number of times people tell me that it worked for them.

But—and hear me out—simply stating what your goal is doesn't necessarily mean you will achieve it. Some of you may disagree with me, but in all my years of experience, this is what I've learned: You must set *realistic* goals. You can maybe have stretch goals, but not ones that truly feel out of reach and discourage you. No pie-in-the-sky aspirations. You need to be clear, focused, and realistic. This also means no affirmation theory that has you repeating phrases like, "I'm a millionaire." You can look in the mirror and tell yourself you're a millionaire all you want, but what is your subconscious mind doing? Go to your mirror now and say you're a millionaire and listen to what your inner dialogue says.

I bet your inner dialogue said, "No, you're not." (Unless you are, of course!) Instead, reframe the goal to be achievable with a bit of a stretch. You may say, "I'm *willing* to make $100,000 a year." Or "I'm *willing* to be a graphic designer. I don't know how I'm going to do it yet, but I'm willing to do what it takes." This triggers the RAS to figure out how to do it. "I'm willing to take on this cause. I'm willing to get others engaged. I may not know how, but I'm going to figure it out."

Out of the Comfort Zone: When Change Isn't Your Idea

When I was eighteen, I was scooping ice cream to make some extra money. As was my tendency then, I thought I was the manager, even though I wasn't. I felt as though people weren't being served fast enough, so on my shift, I tried to get a system in place, even though I had no idea how to run an ice cream store.

Needless to say, after three weeks, I was unceremoni-ously booted out the door, and quite rightly so! While I may have thought my ideas were good (and who knows, maybe they were), I certainly had no idea how to share my ideas in a way that sparked people to action. I had tried to make change happen, and change did happen... but not the kind I wanted or expected! While I was secretly glad to have been fired, it still took me some time to process it, as I hadn't initiated it. If I'd made the choice to leave the job, I wouldn't have spent energy thinking about it and being generally ticked off!

When I speak to people about change, I'm not that interested in how they handle change that is *their* idea or change they agree with. That's because we all respond much more easily to that kind of change than we do to changes we may consider disruptive. When changes are our idea, we're ready to jump on them right away; we're ready to act on them. In fact, we've probably thought them through in our heads a little bit. We like our ideas because we've already lived with them a bit.

We respond very differently to change that's disruptive, which can be ideas that come from another person, or change that comes from someone you don't like, that happens to you from an external source, that you don't instigate, or that's imposed by a person above you on the corporate ladder. Change can also be regulatory, legislative, or governmental.

COVID-19 is a great example of something imposed on us that no one wanted. When it began to build in early 2020, it took us a while during the first few weeks to really wrap our heads around what the hell was going on. (Some of us are still doing that!) And what it showed is that we are more ready for change than we think. One minute we were at our desks; the next, we were figuring out how to juggle work from our kitchen tables with kids, pets, meals, and, of course, the fear that goes along with the unknown. Things we'd taken for granted—our entertainment, communities, workplaces, ability to move around and see friends—experienced significant shifts. But we also learned that we were much better equipped for change than we had imagined. Things we thought would take years to implement, like a totally home-based workplace, were established and functional within weeks. Organizations that normally would've taken years planning how to make their organization virtual, and another year to actually implement the ability to work at home, went virtual in three weeks. I heard it countless times in the sessions I spoke at.

The one gift I've found during this pandemic—if there is one—is that each of us has developed new knowledge, skills, and practices that can help us navigate the future and break through limitations we set on ourselves.

You broke through your own limitations to make it this far. You can engage others more than you think. You can spark action in others. You can lead change that matters to you. And now you're getting to know yourself better than you thought.

The next step is knowing that you'll never know it all, and you don't have to. You won't have all the answers. Engaging others in change is a dialogue, not a one-way information dump. The people you're talking to or engaging with may have answers you didn't even know you needed. It's important to maintain what you want to be heard about, but also to be open to ideas about how to get there and open to insights from the people you're talking with. Everyone has different priorities. To create change that matters, you must realize that your priority won't necessarily be the priority of others.

You'll accomplish all this not by resisting or trying to master change, but by being an apprentice to change.

TALKING POINTS

- Choose your words consciously to program your mindset.

- Watch out for what activates your amygdala.

- Pay attention to your inner dialogue.

- Program your reticular activating system to direct your focus for faster results.

- You can adapt and move forward when you're out of your comfort zone.

3

Be an Apprentice to Change

"In every encounter or experience, there is the potential for gaining our enlightenment, the possibility of finding that one missing piece of the puzzle that brings about illumination. It is our own mind that determines the experience."

MASAAKI HATSUMI, thirty-fourth ninja grandmaster

F THE GLOBAL PANDEMIC has taught us one thing, it is that while we may think we are in control of our work and personal lives, the world is unpredictable, and we must learn to roll with the punches. No matter how accomplished we are, how much we have learned, or how long we have been in a leadership role, we are not masters of change. Change is the master, and we are its apprentices.

The ability to adapt and change in times of uncertainty and economic downturn can mean the difference between falling behind the competition and leading the pack. The reality is that much of your success will come from planning (for example, carefully selecting attainable goals, and determining the way you communicate the change to the people you want to engage), but the rest of your success will come from the opposite of planning: that is, from your ability to adjust and shift as needed.

Another thing the global crisis taught me, as I worked internationally with organizations that were going through the pandemic, is that many ideas I believed about how we initiate and respond to change were not true!

There are myths of change I have had to unlearn—and you need to unlearn them too.

When you say goodbye to the following six change management myths, you will significantly improve your efforts in engaging others in your ideas to effect change.

Myth 1: Change Is Hard

Individuals vary, of course, and some people find change more difficult than others. However, the more you can prepare yourself and others, the easier change will be. This requires formulating a solid plan for enacting that change, which includes a strategy for communication, action planning, training, and ongoing support. Even changes we are prepared for may take effort, but that is not the same thing as being hard, let alone impossible, to achieve. Apprenticeship to change is work, but it builds your skill.

Myth 2: When It Comes to Change, People Need Time to Grieve

This can be true in some circumstances—for example, in processing the death of a loved one, leaving your old home for a new one, or switching to a new job. However, when we are talking about workplace ideas or changes such as process improvements or software upgrades that don't impact you on a deep level, you can eliminate the grieving period simply by being *ready* for change.

Yes, there will be personal impact, but nothing that will necessarily touch you in an emotional way. Deciding to change how you are going to do a complex process doesn't usually involve a fear of loss or grief for people. Yes, they may have been comfortable before, and it will be uncomfortable now, but time won't be wasted mourning the loss of the old process. Preparing for change involves fully understanding how the change will impact each individual, the team, or the community, and supporting them as they migrate to new ideas, actions, systems, procedures, or operations.

Myth 3: To Deal With Change, We Must Know What the Future Holds

We like knowing how the future will unfold. That's why many of us read horoscopes, consult tarot cards, or go to fortune tellers, even if it's just for fun. Wouldn't it be nice if we could know what the future holds? In the work world, we create business plans, strategic plans, action plans, communication plans—they are the tarot cards of business. And just as with tarot cards, the plans often don't unroll the way we wanted them to... for good or bad!

Unfortunately, no one can predict the future, and this goes for businesses that have been doing things the same way for decades as well as those who are blazing new trails with their innovative ideas.

Of course, when you have an idea on which you want people to take action, you want to be able to tell them how it will impact the future based on your best research or predictions. The same applies when you decide on a change in your organization: you are putting a stake in the sand. However, in both cases, you always have to be open to altering those ideas and adjusting when necessary. Remember: you can navigate change, but you cannot control it.

Think about when you plan a trip. You figure out where you want to go, buy your airline tickets, and book your accommodation. You plan for places you want to see (I'm partial to art galleries and museums!) and get ready for takeoff. And then you get to the airport and your flight is delayed. You start to get a bit nervous. Eventually, you get on your flight and land at your destination—and guess what? Your trip doesn't go 100 percent as planned. The museum has to close due to a flood, the concert you came to see is canceled because the performer is sick, and traffic is terrible in the city where you landed.

These are situations beyond your control. The success of your vacation is dependent on how you respond to and navigate these changes. Besides, the future doesn't always bring bad things! Maybe the museum you want to see is open, but (because you are open to new ideas and you are "change-ready") you decide at the last minute you'd rather go see a nearby castle instead. You didn't know about the castle before, but once you found out, you weren't chained to your original plan. You were ready to help a good change happen—as an apprentice should be.

Myth 4: Lofty and Ambitious Change Goals Are Good

Having something to strive toward is an excellent moti-
vator in life as well as in business. That said, reaching
too high all at once in your change goals can demotivate
you and the people you are trying to engage in your idea.
Goals that are unrealistic and perceived as out of reach
can trigger that impending feeling of failure from the
start. You won't be sparking any action by doing that!

Years ago, my boss at the agency where I worked read
a book that suggested that setting completely unrealistic
goals would result in you being very happy rather than
dissatisfied when you met only 50 percent of them. At
the next staff meeting, my boss identified for everyone
a huge number of unreachable goals—like, SO OUT OF
REACH, THERE WAS NO WAY ANYONE COULD EVER
ACCOMPLISH THEM! (All caps intended!) My team
opted out completely and said they couldn't participate
in the program because the goals were unreachable.

I still dislike that book intensely, mostly because of my
boss' interpretation of it. But also, the concept behind
that book goes against all the performance psychology
I've ever read. My experience—and what the research
shows—is that we need to set goals we can see ourselves
reaching. I'm all for stretch goals as well—but as I mentioned earlier, they can't be too far out of reach. We have
to believe we can do them or we will lose the drive and
motivation to do it.

If you have a large goal, a better strategy is to break it
into smaller goals that can be added incrementally. Use

the S.M.A.R.T. protocol: make sure each goal is specific, measurable, achievable/attainable, relevant, and time-specific.

Myth 5: Resistance Is Bad

When you announce an idea you are passionate about—or a change you'd like to accomplish in your business or organization—you may find that some people are resistant to that change. This is normal, and it can give you valuable information if you are willing to listen.

Like you, I don't actually like to have to deal with negativity or resistance. Who has time for that? Yet what I've learned is that if I can find out why people are resistant to my idea, I can formulate an even better plan to get them engaged.

Dealing with resistance doesn't mean you have to necessarily solve the problem for the individual. Take the pressure off yourself! Research shows that just acknowledging someone's problems and hearing them out can ease their resistance and bring them closer to embracing your ideas and the change you want to implement. According to experts Guy Itzchakov and Avi Kluger, "listening seems to make an employee more relaxed, more self-aware of his or her strengths and weaknesses, and more willing to reflect in a non-defensive manner."

By listening, you will gain valuable insight into how your change impacts various individuals. It also allows you a chance to engage with your audience meaningfully, so you can harness their energy and spark them to action. And you don't need to sell them or convince them about your idea! Your goal is just to create an open and safe environment in which they can engage with you and hear about your ideas. Trying to convince someone your idea is right will only lead to frustration. You don't need to be the master at all times; you are, after all, an apprentice to change. And that means having a dialogue, not a one-way conversation.

Myth 6: Change Should Always Be Packaged as Positive

Ugh. The tyranny of positive thinking. While I believe positive thinking is important, it's often used at the wrong time. When that happens, it leaves a bad taste in everyone's mouth. Overlooking the negative aspects of your ideas will make people think you are out of touch with reality and haven't thought things through. You need to be aware of the weaknesses and potential negative consequences of your plans, anticipate what people's objections will be, and address them head-on.

Years ago, I worked with a colleague whom I'll call Richard. Richard worked in community outreach and was excellent at his job. He knew how to engage others in his ideas and could rally people to take action. But Richard was at a crossroads in his life. His past work in community outreach and then consulting didn't let him use his gifts and talents the way he really wanted to.

Richard's real passion was interior design. He wanted to bring his skills in creating community to interior design, so he opened an interior design business without any formal training. He used his community outreach experience with clients to truly understand what they wanted.

What could be negative about that? As noted above, we have to anticipate what people's objections to our ideas might be and then address them directly. The biggest obstacle was the perceived lack of formal training. Richard could not walk into a meeting and present his lack of formal training as a positive. In our work together, we had to anticipate the perfectly reasonable objections he might face.

To compensate, Richard developed a portfolio of his designs, worked on getting into some media and magazines (for credibility purposes), and addressed potential negative perceptions head-on. Years later, he is still using his community outreach experience to engage others and thus design truly meaningful spaces for his clients.

To best effect change, don't try to convince people your ideas will work unless you address the negative aspects too. Stick to the facts and be honest. Identify concerns, address them head-on, and be prepared to answer questions. Sentences that start with "At least..." (for example, "At least I've been in these magazines") are cues that you may be trying to put a positive spin on things instead of confronting the downsides of the change. We'll look at addressing the potential downsides of change in much more depth in chapter 9, when we talk about analyzing the impact of our suggested change on those whose action we are trying to instigate.

TALKING POINTS

- Change is the master, so be a good apprentice to it. You can always learn.

- Change doesn't have to be hard, and if you're ready for it, you don't always need a "grieving" period when it happens.

- You don't need to know what the future holds.

- Make your goals ambitious but not unrealistic.

- When there is resistance, listen to deeply understand why.

- Don't get stuck in the tyranny of positive thinking and sugarcoat the downsides. Address them head-on.

4

Lead at the Edge of Change

"At this level everyone knows how to play tennis... The thing that separates the best from the rest is just the mindset."

BIANCA ANDREESCU, professional tennis player

WHY DOES it seem as though certain people respond to and go through change better than others? Because they have developed the skills and beliefs they need to lead through the change. But these skills and beliefs are things everyone can learn and practice. Everyone can be a leader, regardless of job title, past experience, education, or where they were born. Having the job title doesn't make someone a leader. I've worked with CEOs who aren't great leaders and administrative professionals who are!

Change requires us to expand the vision of who we are and what we, our communities, our teams, and our organizations, can do. To spark action and lead through change, we must ask this question: If I'm willing to let go of the reality that is predictable, what is possible in the unknown?

Living in the unknown creates possibility, and possibility gives you opportunities to innovate, create, and experience something new. Change has many lessons to teach, and when we ignore them, we miss out on the chance to grow and become more of who we are meant to be. When we embrace change as an opportunity to see things differently and reach different outcomes, we build different qualities, skills, and practices. Your willingness to be an apprentice to change will greatly strengthen your capacity to lead others through your ideas and through change.

In fact, when you take ownership and fully step into the apprentice role, you will understand how truly magical change can be. Imagine transforming your ideas into action in your business, community, department, or role, or in a social cause that is deeply meaningful to you. Imagine knowing that the next time life throws you a curveball, you have confidence in your ability to knock it out of the park. Sure, predictability feels safe, but it also creates limitations. Change opens the door to possibility. Step through!

And no matter how you wish other people or situations to change, all change starts internally: always begin with yourself. These next insights will help you develop your own ability to change before you guide others.

Insight 1: Start with the Right Mindset (The Most Important Thing Ever to Do!)

In the quote at the beginning of this chapter, Bianca Andreescu tells us what separates good tennis players from the best: mindset. You can substitute tennis player with any profession or role you like: entrepreneur, coach, leader, community activist, accountant, speaker, whatever.

I introduced the topic of mindset in chapter 2 and I'm coming back to it now because it's especially important. If you program your mindset the right way, it will respond efficiently. Instead of painting a negative picture of the future, paint a more positive, factual one.

Nearly every day before I get out of bed, I thank my bed for a good sleep. (I really do—there are more than a billion people on the planet who don't have a comfortable bed. How lucky am I?!) After working in health care for years, I'm honestly quite grateful to actually wake up in the morning! After all, the alternative is *not* waking up. That may sound trite, but this simple act of gratitude works for me and the research backs this up. This prompts my brain to keep looking for the good. Next, I pat my cat on the back and say, "Today is going to be a really good day." Because most likely it will be.

Now, my life doesn't unfold with roses, lollipops, and rainbows. And I'm definitely *not* a Pollyanna. Bad things happen and, yes, things don't go always go my way. But when I program my mindset with positivity in the morning, I'm generally in a better frame of mind to handle the bad things when they happen.

This is essential because when you set your mindset and beliefs about a topic in advance, your behaviors and even reality will often follow. This phenomenon is known as the self-fulfilling prophecy: "a belief or expectation that an individual holds about a future event that manifests because the individual holds it." Unconsciously, you may work to affirm your belief—which is why it is vital to start with a positive mindset.

Negative thought patterns are normal and even natural during a period of crisis. It's also normal if Insight 2 (below) makes you feel a little uncomfortable. But you need to recognize when negativity is creeping in so you can address the thoughts and move on from them. Let your confidence come not from knowing exactly what will happen next, but rather from believing in your ability to handle it no matter what. Your confidence comes from your past successes—of which you likely have many.

Insight 2: Accept That You Won't Have All the Answers

Thinking that you must know what the future holds to successfully lead a change or an initiative is Change Management Myth 3 (see chapter 3 for the six myths). As I said, no one can predict the future; you can navigate change, but you cannot control it. From this, simple logic tells you that you can't have all the answers.

Now, obviously, you would not be here reading this if you didn't want to help people. In general, we tend to assume that helping people means having answers for them. We want to remove roadblocks, give advice, problem-solve, and generally make people's lives better. But one thing I've learned—and my guess is, you probably have too—is that you need to be at peace with the fact that you can't remove everyone's problems or make their lives less busy, less complex, smoother, and so on.

What you *can* do most of the time is listen to their issues and acknowledge them. As we've already seen in

Change Management Myth 5, acknowledging issues will move people down the path of change often as much as actually solving their problems.

When I had an office with an actual wall many years ago, I had three questions up on the wall to guide discussions when people came in with a problem—questions I still often use in discussions:

- Do you want me to solve it?

- Do you want me to help you solve it?

- Do you want me just to listen?

What do you think I wanted to do? Solve the issue! What do you think my team members wanted me to do most of the time? Listen!

Insight 3: Make Decisions Even Without All the Information

It's easy to become paralyzed by uncertainty. As an apprentice to change, you may not always have the expertise or knowledge to deal with a particular situation, but you still need to make decisions, step up, and take action frequently.

One of the things I learned from working virtually with people all around the world during COVID-19 was that regardless of what role they had in their organization, they had to make the best decisions they could with the information they had at the time. That was my own experience too. I had to narrow my focus and look at what I could control and make decisions about. And I had to do that knowing things might change.

This can be difficult, as you may be waiting for all the information to make the best decision possible. But use your professional judgment. Gather the best data available to you and take small, simple, manageable steps to move your ideas forward.

Have you ever said, "I wish someone would make a decision"? Well, that someone just might be you!

Insight 4: Build New "Human Resource" Capabilities

The qualities that make a good apprentice to change are solid "human resources" to have in any situation. By human resources here, I'm not referring to staff and employees. I'm talking about the human qualities, skills, or practices you may need.

Human resource qualities, including compassion and empathy, are keys to successfully engaging others in your ideas and leading them through the change you want to see happen. Getting into the mind of each person helps you understand the impact the change will have on them. Apprentices to change are also naturally curious and want to explore the world around them. Their strength comes not from knowing exactly what to do, but from being willing to gather diverse opinions from those around them to find the best solution.

Each idea we want to implement, each change situation, requires our presence, wisdom, knowledge, and discernment to create the magic of change we know is possible.

Insight 5: Lead Alongside Your Team

Some leaders are in front of their teams, pulling them toward their vision; others are the quiet guide at the back slowly showing people the way forward. But I would argue that most times it is best for you to lead alongside your team toward the change you want to implement. You are experiencing the change at the same time. You are responding to your ideas at the same time. You are all apprentices to change, learning from the change—just in different roles.

Leading alongside your team puts you in the mindset that you are all in this together. That removes the pressure of you having to know all the answers, as I mentioned in Insight 2. When you lead alongside your team, it allows you to show your humanity in the situation, which in turn builds trust. When you admit that you don't have all the answers and that you are uncertain about some situations, and when you demonstrate empathy toward others who are experiencing your ideas as change, you show that you are in the trenches with them, that while you may be leading the way, you are supporting them and yourself at the same time.

TALKING POINTS

- Always start with the right mindset.

- You won't have all the answers, and that's okay. (Read that again.)

- You can make decisions without all the information.

- Develop and demonstrate compassion and empathy.

- Lead alongside your team and let your humanity show. You're in this together.

5

Cocreate Change

"I know of no single formula for success, but over the years I have observed that some attributes of leadership are universal and are often about finding ways of encouraging people to combine their efforts, their talents, their insights, their enthusiasm and their inspiration to work together."

QUEEN ELIZABETH II TO THE UNITED NATIONS, 2010

A S I WAS RUNNING A BUSINESS and trying to figure out my life (as we all were) during the COVID-19 lockdowns, the side of me that needs to be around and talk to people was really suffering. As a raging extrovert, I found myself yearning for connection. Even though I had friends around me and, thankfully, someone I lived with, work-wise, there was no one anymore!

I started to set up monthly calls with a few colleagues whose opinions I valued. I took on projects such as updating my website, newsletter, and other items. I realized I couldn't just sit, isolated, in my office. I had to work with others to cocreate the future I wanted. It sounds simple, but during the pandemic, it wasn't as easy to remember. There was so much big change happening on the planet.

Now more than ever, I am certain that we can't do things alone—and we can't create change that matters solely by ourselves. And when we're leading change, as we just saw in Insight 5 in chapter 4, we need to lead not from the front or back but *alongside* our team. Whether we are initially on our own and trying to engage others in our ideas or working in an organization with a team, we are alongside others.

A note on terminology: Going forward, I'm going to use the word "team." If you are in an organization, that may refer to the people who report to you or whom you work with. If you are trying to spark action and create change outside of that more formal structure, your team may be made up of a friend who is helping you, a book-keeper, the person you see at the bank, a social media guru, and/or a colleague you bounce ideas off of. A team can be made up of anyone who supports you in creating the change that matters to you.

Here are four tactics you can use to be heard and to cocreate change.

Tactic 1: Build Trust by Using Clear Language

When we use clear language and hold others account-able for using similar language, we build trust. Determine what is the appropriate language your team needs to hear and use it to engage them in the process of change.

Remember, when we are under pressure, we fre-quently use language that isn't accurate and can some-times be exaggerated. (I know I can sometimes!) If you receive a report that has a few errors in it, do you say, "It's a disaster"? Or do you say, "It has a few errors in it"? Rationally, you know it has a few errors, but if you are under pressure to deliver it to your executive team, a project team, or—for those of you in the public sector—the city council, this language may slip in! But it erodes trust: it provokes a defensive response, and it shows you as playing a little loose with the truth.

Similarly, when someone has an issue, don't minimize it with your language. For example, if you use the term "first world problems" when someone else is having an issue they consider serious, it diminishes their experience. (More on this in chapter 8!) It's not always appropriate to set the context or help people get perspective when they are in the middle of something stressful. Instead, find out what you can do to help.

As I said earlier, when you are leading alongside others, you are experiencing the same uncertainty about the future and discomfort with not knowing all the answers. Letting your team know that you are in this with them can be the greatest gift you give them. They will not feel alone. You all become part of the same team then. So tell them.

Tactic 2: Focus on Purpose and Priorities

I have found the following three questions effective in instilling purpose and focus in your team when you are in the throes of trying to get them to take action. Ask these questions weekly to build momentum and create focus. They do work!

1 **What** two accomplishments are you most proud of this week? (You can use any number; I'll often use one accomplishment.)

2 **Why** were they important to you? (This is the most important part; it instills purpose. You can't say,

"Because my boss said so," or "I was on a deadline."
You must identify a reason other than that.)

3 **What** will you do to continue the momentum next
week? (This builds focus.)

When you focus on purpose and why you're doing the
work you do, it's easy to adjust your plans.

Henry was a young, successful interior designer who
owned his own firm, but he really wanted to know what
his higher purpose was on the planet. A very common
refrain—I've asked myself the same, and I've heard it
from many others. As his coach, I told Henry what I've
learned: that our higher purpose isn't *out there*, somewhere in the universe to be found. It's about how we feel
when *we* are "on purpose."

How do you know when you're "on purpose"? You feel
it. It's not an intellectual exercise. Think back to a time
when you were "in the zone"—for example, you lost track
of time when you were working on something meaningful, being your best self, or contributing to others...
whatever comes to mind. What did it feel like?

I know I'm "on purpose" when I'm onstage in front of
a group of people and I'm totally in the flow of what I'm
saying and how I'm interacting with the audience. I also
feel I'm in my zone when I'm working one-on-one with
others. Not all the time, but when it's *good*. It feels time-
less. I feel connected. I feel I'm contributing to the greater
whole among others. I feel useful as I'm helping others.

After you've identified what it feels like to you when
you're in the zone, I'd like to gently—well, actually,
firmly—suggest you start making a list, on your mobile

phone or a piece of paper, of every time for the next week you felt like you were "on purpose."

You should end up with a list that is specific to you, but it may look something like the following.

I felt "on purpose" when:

- I walked my dog through the park and stopped to help an elderly person get off a bench.

- I had a great staff meeting where the team just jelled.

- I applied for a mortgage and felt really good that I got it.

- I helped someone improve their business.

- Someone thanked me for writing that article.

- I stood up for my team member in front of a rude customer.

When you start documenting all the times you felt "on purpose," you will soon find that your higher purpose reveals itself. But not only that: you may have many higher purposes! And they may unfold at different times.

When you focus on the purpose and priorities of what's happening, you'll realize your higher purpose isn't out there somewhere but right inside you, revealing itself step by step.

Tactic 3: Prepare Your Team to Be Unprepared

As everyone knows, getting people engaged in your ideas isn't a stagnant process. We must stay open, learn, and adapt as we go. This is relevant whether you are an entrepreneur, a coach, an employee or a business owner, or a leader. For many reasons, people you try to spur to action will differ in their ability to successfully navigate the changes. It is important to identify key members of your team who will help facilitate change for others. Find people who love your ideas—or are at least open to them and willing to take off with them. They are your "change all-stars" who have stepped up to the plate.

Going through the COVID-19 pandemic has forced all of us to become more accepting of and comfortable with ambiguity and uncertainty. Like many, I had to cancel events and trips I had planned, particularly during the initial period as we went into lockdown. I watched the news and became completely overwhelmed by what was going on—as I'm sure many of you also did. Everything seemed unpredictable.

I realized that to deal with all this I had to narrow my focus to what I had control over during the day. So I developed a new structure and routine. I walked instead of going to the gym, set up Zoom meetings with friends, and so on. Professionally, I asked people what skills they'd developed through the pandemic, and they identified their ability to be resilient, develop new skills with technology, and prioritize.

These skills can be applied to any challenge in the future. We just need to be reminded that we've developed them. Helping people narrow their focus to what they have control over in the short term will, in turn, help them feel comfortable with ambiguity in the longer term.

When they identify the qualities and skills they've used to deal with ambiguity in the past, they will be better prepared to be unprepared.

Tactic 4: Break Through Self-Imposed Limitations

I mentioned this in chapter 1 of this book, and it bears repeating here: our self-imposed limitations are our greatest barrier to change.

One of the quickest ways to identify limitations is to listen for the word "because." When someone says, "We can't do this *because...*" everything after the word "because" is generally a limitation.

How many of you have heard someone say they can't do something because

* it won't work here,
* they don't have experience,
* they're too old,
* they're too young,
* they don't have a degree,
* they can't change quickly enough, or
* they don't have the money or the time?

All of these examples and others can usually be disproved in some way. Gather evidence or proof of other situations or people, communities, or organizations that have done something similar (it doesn't need to be exact).

When you are able to show evidence of someone else accomplishing the change you want, you remove doubt.

As cultural anthropologist Angeles Arrien often said, "That which we witness, we are forever changed by, and once witnessed we can never go back." When you remove doubt, you give yourself and others the courage needed to step into the future and work together to create change that matters.

You cannot make change happen on your own. The process of cocreating with others is where you will find success. The bonus is, cocreation also helps you with new ideas, team unity, and diversity, and—one of the best parts—it ramps up your idea to influence others and you can get more done. When you remember to lead alongside others and cocreate with them, you engage them in your ideas to create change that matters—that's when the spark happens!

TALKING POINTS

- Weave others into your ideas.
- Use clear language to build trust.
- Focus on purpose and priorities.
- Be prepared to be unprepared.
- Break through your self-imposed limitations.

6

Shape the Future

"X never, ever, marks the spot."

INDIANA JONES (and on his quest, X does mark the spot!)

DO YOU REMEMBER the part in the 1989 movie *Indiana Jones and the Last Crusade* where Indiana had to cross a huge chasm with no apparent way to do so? He had spent time researching and uncovering what he should do to get the Holy Grail, and he realized he needed to take a calculated risk: a "leap of faith." All the signs had led him to this point. He had put all the information together. On the edge of the chasm, he took a giant step, dangling his foot out into the open air, and then stepped down. Instead of plummeting into the depths below, he ended up finding solid ground! Taking that risk and moving step by step across the path allowed him to reach the treasure on the other side.

Stepping into the unknown is what we are all required to do when we are trying to get others to engage in our ideas to spark action. Just like Indiana in the chapter-opening quote, we may be so sure of our answer, yet just as he learns later, we have to be flexible and realize that maybe "X" really does mark the spot. We have to take calculated risks—and we have to help the people we're engaging take calculated risks.

There are six steps you must take to achieve this. (Hopefully, you won't need to cross any chasms in your quest to get your ideas out!) Being heard and engaging others in your ideas so they can take action will require you to shift, expand, and innovate the way you and others see your idea. To get others engaged in your idea, you and the people you are talking with must process change first internally and then externally: once you have done it for yourself (the internal work), then you can illuminate the path for others with whom you want to cocreate (the external work). This means you have six steps in total—three (shift, expand, innovate) times two (internal, external).

Shift

The first two steps require you and the people you want to engage to mentally pivot and view your ideas in a new light.

1. Internal: Shift Your Mindset

Shaping the future you want will require you first to realize there is no "new normal" for the world we live and work in. Things constantly change. I think there are going to be a bunch of "new normals" that will keep shifting in the next few years. It is important to not get your mind set on any one path forward. We've already gotten started on shifting mindset (see chapters 2 and 3).

2. External: Analyze the Ecosystem

This is the first external process you do. Once you've adopted a mindset of change and flexibility, then you can do the external analysis.

Analyzing your ecosystem is more than just an environmental scan of your external surroundings. I use the term "ecosystem" purposefully. An "environmental scan" tells you, "This is what's going on." When I say "ecosystem," I also want you to look at the interrelationships of everything. How does everything relate? How are things held together? How do things work together? This involves looking at your idea holistically—the people, the leaders, the personalities, the mindsets, the history, the processes, the technology... in sum, the entire context of what you are asking people to do.

What is the most important part of the ecosystem that you need to consider moving forward to create change that matters?

Expand

Once you've shifted your mindset and analyzed your ecosystem, you're ready to expand your thinking and examine new ways of getting your ideas across so you can truly create the change that matters to you on the planet.

3. Internal: Be Open to Ideas

Expanding your thinking means being open to systems, ideas, and processes you may not have considered before.

Or ideas you may think are disruptive. Or that you think can't work.

The late Virginia Satir, a popular family therapist, was reported to have done a study on dishwashing. She called it her "Silly Study." She found that there were more than 250 different ways to do dishes and load the dishwasher—250! Who knew?! Now here's the most interesting part to me: every single person thought their way was the right way!

If there are more than 250 different ways to load the dishwasher and do dishes, then just maybe there is another way to do that business process, or share your idea, or accomplish your goal. Maybe your way isn't the best way. Maybe someone else has the answer. If we open and expand our thinking, new ideas, tips, and techniques may come. There are usually many ways to accomplish a goal. So remember the dishwashing! (As a bonus, if you want to learn how to stop trying to control every outcome, practice not moving dishes around in the dishwasher after someone else loads it.)

Making a major shift may sound like it will be time-consuming. However, an interesting lesson that the pandemic has taught us (which I've mentioned already) is that getting your ideas out and compelling people to take action on them may not take as much time as you think. I'm not saying by any means that you should rush things. What I am saying is to be aware of any limitations you put out there about what ideas to express and how much time it will take.

It does take practice to expand your thinking, of course. The practice of expanding your thinking will allow you to break through old mental models and inspire innovation in how you think and act. Use perspective to your advantage. You probably didn't think you'd accomplish the impossible and make it through the last few years, yet here you are.

Take a moment and ask yourself this question: What seems impossible to me now that just might be possible?

4. External: Plan Diverse Approaches

This is often people's favorite step, yet if you want to engage others in new ideas, spark action, *and* lead change that matters, you do have to do the previous three steps first!

In step 1, you opened your mind to possibilities. In step 2, you analyzed your current ecosystem. Having that information, in step 3 you expanded your thinking to harness new ideas. Now you can think about the many different paths you can take to accomplish your goal. Let's get the planning going!

First, a note about planning: Don't get stuck on the "right way." Plans need to be nimble, agile, and able to be executed within a short time. As things move forward, be ready to change course at a moment's notice.

To help you do this, get very clear on what your specific purpose is with your plan. Is it to create X? Do Y? Make the world a better place? When you focus your energy on a specific purpose, you can adjust quickly to get the greatest results when changes arise—and they will.

To focus on purpose, ask the right questions. The word "question" is related to the word "quest," which is the start of a journey. What journey do you want to start people on? The right questions can guide that journey.

For example, if you ask, "What did you accomplish last week?" you will get a list of things that someone did. But if you then ask, "Why was that important to you?" you go deeper by asking the person to focus on their purpose and priorities.

When you plan the journey, think of the Paris Métro. Paris is one of my favorite cities in the world to visit—I love the people, the food, the culture, the fact one can have champagne at most meals—and one of the best parts of Paris is the Métro: their subway system. Wherever you are in Paris, if you look at the Métro map, you'll see that it gives you many different ways to get to the same place. For example, if I am leaving my hotel near the Place de la Concorde and want to get to the famous shopping area at Les Halles, the simplest way to get there is line 1. The Louvre is two stops past Concorde and Les Halles is just a bit farther. But if for some reason line 1 is down, I can take at least three other obvious alternative routes to get there. While it may take longer in some cases, and require a few stops, I can still get to Les Halles and go shopping!

As you start to plan how you will engage others in your ideas and spur them to action, identify the easiest way to get there. Then ask: What are the alternative plans I could use to accomplish my goal? Usually, there are a few!

Innovate

A shifted mindset and expanded ideas will allow you to shape the future to create something new that maybe you didn't have before, or reinvent a new way of doing something.

5. Internal: Take a Risk

Now comes the hard part: taking action. To take action, first, we have to deal with our own worries and the worries of others. View your worries as risks—and manage them! You do it all the time without even knowing it: If you're worried about being hit by a car when you cross the street, you look both ways to make sure no cars are coming. You leave two hours early for the airport to keep from missing your flight. And if you're going to jump off a cliff, you make sure you have a parachute. I mean that figuratively, but I also mean it literally—I've jumped off mountains, and you'd better believe I had a properly packed parachute on my back!

I've told you this before, and I'll tell you again: *Worries are just made-up negative stories.* Now, I'm not saying "don't listen to people's worries." Listen! Absolutely. However, in the context of engaging others to take action and of creating change on the planet, we want to ground worries in facts to help people manage them. For example, if you are worried people will react negatively to your idea, you can ask questions to ground this in fact and develop a plan to deal with it.

Ask yourself, "What is the likelihood of this happening?" and "What can I do to reduce the chance of it happening or to prevent it from happening?" (Don't be too quick to say "nothing." There's usually *something* you can do to prevent or reduce the impact.) Also ask, "If it does happen, how does it impact what I'm trying to do?

What's my plan B?" After all, if you are planning an out-door barbecue and you're worried it's going to rain, do you just stand around waiting for it to rain? I think you don't. I *hope* you don't!

You can't manage all worries and risks, but by focusing on ones that have a higher likelihood of happening, you can create plans to manage them so you feel confident you have things handled should anything go awry. Doesn't that feel good? No last-minute panic. Breathe. I like that.

You're ready to take risks. So let's get to the last step.

6. External: Create the New

Getting people to take action on your ideas isn't always easy. Wouldn't it be great if it was? It means more external *action*! So, what is the new behavior, skill, technology, business, or community you want to create? Now is the time to do what Indiana Jones did and take the leap of faith.

To help you do this:

- **Don't generate ideas (creative thinking) and make decisions (critical thinking) at the same time, as it won't bring about new ideas.** We've all been to those meetings where new ideas pop up but get shut down the next minute. Nothing gets accomplished. Then you have to have another meeting to figure out what happened at the last meeting! Who has time for that? Clearly state on your meeting agenda how much time is allotted for idea generation and how much is for determining which ideas you will act on. Make sure there is a clear distinction between them. This gives all possibilities and suggestions a chance and, most importantly, allows innovation to occur.

- **As you go forward, balance emotional responses with the facts.** The unknown can create fear and cause us to say no to something purely for emotional reasons. There are also valid emotional responses. Balance the emotional responses (don't dismiss or discard them) with the facts. Is there any evidence or proof that other people or organizations have done something similar and experienced success?

- **Watch what goes into your brain as you start your day.** Don't watch, listen to, or read the news for the first hour—it will impact your mindset and ability to make decisions throughout the day.

As you know, the future of your work is probably going to be different from what you imagined. Normal is gone! Uncertainty is here to stay. Remember that it's the magic of daily changes that will create the biggest difference in the quality of your life and work. Incorporate the six steps listed above into your daily change practices. Who knows what great things you might create!

Now you have your change plan. The next thing is to speak it into being: tell the story that will spark action to make it happen.

TALKING POINTS

- Shift your mindset and look at how you can shift your ecosystem.

- Be open to ideas and plan diverse approaches.

- Allow ideas to collide for innovation to occur.

- Translate worries into risks.

- Take a risk and go boldly forth to spark action.

7

Design the Story You Will Tell

"There's a story behind everything. How a picture got on a wall. How a scar got on your face. Sometimes the stories are simple, and sometimes they are hard."
MITCH ALBOM

STORYTELLING IS important if you want to create change that matters. You may sigh and ask, "Why can't I just tell them how great this idea is and get on with it?" It would be wonderful if you could, but cold, dry facts don't always do the trick on their own. People care about facts when they are connected to things that interest them. You have to be strategic in bringing your ideas of change to people and include stories that help the information come alive. Effective storytelling takes your ideas and weaves them into a narrative that can be impactful and create change that matters. Both information and stories need to exist side by side to engage others in your ideas so they take action on them.

There are many different frameworks for telling stories, and at the most basic level, they follow the simple process of an introduction, a body, and a conclusion. Most importantly, when you're telling stories to effect change, you will connect better with your audience if they hear or see something they can relate to, such as a person or similar situation that is relevant to the audience. Next, what was the turning point for them during the process of change, and finally, what was the outcome for the person or the situation? What change happened as a result of taking action?

In this chapter, I'm going to cover the big-picture basics of analyzing and structuring a story. And then in the next few chapters, we're going to add more depth and details for putting your story into action to help you be a creator and leader of change.

Story Analysis

Let's warm up your mental muscles by analyzing a story you currently tell.

1 Identify a work-related story that you tell people or a story that's related to your business, volunteer work, committee work, or activism and advocacy that you've told before.

2 Identify the key points of your story (your content) and how you told it (your delivery).

- How did you tell it before?

- How did you determine what was effective and what wasn't?

- How did you determine what content to include?

- What were the key takeaways for the listener?

- What change happened as a result of you telling the story?

- What feedback did you get? (If you didn't get feedback from it, go tell it to someone now and get some feedback on how compelling it was. Don't make it a family member—make it someone who's going to give you objective feedback, like a colleague, business coach, or a peer.)

- **Pro tip:** Record yourself on your mobile device or on Zoom telling your story. You'll quickly hear what needs to be fine-tuned!

3 Plot the trajectory of the story.

- What was the setting?

- What was the context?

- When did you share who the characters were?

- When did you share the main key point—the big reveal?

- When did you give the takeaways?

- Did this trajectory change depending on your audience? If so, how?

Looking at stories this way helps build a habit of being conscious of what you're telling and how.

Your Topic

Now let's take the topic on which you want to lead change and analyze it in-depth. Then you can determine how to deliver the story in a strategic way.

There are three key questions to ask about the topic:

1. How can this topic or story cause change? What do I want to achieve with this change story? What are the benefits and impacts or challenges of the topic or story?

It's what stories you tell and how you tell them that matters most. Your stories don't need to be big ones to get a good point across. They just need to be vivid, personal, and alive—and, most importantly, framed in a way that will be heard.

2. How will I create dissatisfaction with the status quo while honoring the past? In order to get people to engage in our ideas and act on them, we have to tell them why what is going on now isn't good anymore *and* at the same time be respectful and honor the past that got you there.

I'll show you what I mean. You've probably experienced something similar to this. Many years ago, I had a great boss, "Paul." He supported me, coached me, and let me bring my creativity to my role, as long as it aligned with the goals of our department and organization. But he got offered a better role somewhere else. Don't you just hate when that happens? You're working so well with someone and then, *BAM*, they go! And so "Robert," my new boss, was hired. At the first meeting, he said something to this effect: "The way this department has been working is all wrong. I've been hired to fix this mess and clean it up."

Needless to say, with that message, *none of us* was on board. We knew there were reasons to change, but telling us that we were all basically losers and messed up (which is how we interpreted it) didn't play well. You can't trash-talk the past and expect the people who were involved in it to be gung ho with your ideas!

So how could Robert have created dissatisfaction with the status quo while honoring the past to get us engaged in his ideas so we could take action on the changes that mattered to him? He could have said, "I've been hired to create change. The department has worked well up until now. You've produced good work. Your clients are happy. Yet the way we do our work is changing; technology is changing. We need to look at ways to do even better than we are now. I'm here to help you do that."

If he had done it that way, I can guarantee we would've been much more open to his ideas. Instead, his plans never really took off and he left the job in a year and half. That wasn't the only reason, but respecting the people and ideas that made the organization just wasn't in his leadership repertoire.

3. What will it look like when I resolve these issues or adapt to the change? What is the outcome I want? This should be framed in the positive, not the negative. Martin Luther King Jr. didn't say, "I have a complaint!" He said, "I have a dream."

Your Audience

The change you want happens in the mind of the other person, so now you need to examine your audience. Ask yourself:

- What are the most important strengths the audience currently has that will help with this change?

- What about this topic will people judge negatively?

- How can I frame it from their perspective?

- What is the specific language I can use so they can actually hear me?

- What does the audience need to know, be, do, or have in order to take action?

- What questions may arise? How will I handle them?

We will address all of these points in greater detail in the coming chapters!

Yourself

Finally, let's analyze your relationship to the topic. What about this change makes you uncomfortable? Unsure? Gets your back up? When thinking about the change you want to create, it's essential to also anticipate others' reactions that might make you feel uncomfortable and think about how you will handle them.

Many years ago, when I was in my late twenties, I was presenting at a physicians' conference. I had started the presentation with the research the topic was based on, and I had just finished sharing tips with the audience on how to work with drug users who were living on the street. A physician stood up and started grilling me on where these tips came from and why they should even care. Needless to say, I hadn't anticipated this. I was intimidated and a bit flustered. I restated the research my tips were based on, and thankfully the moderator ended the session.

I realized I never wanted to go through that again. I also was facilitating workshops on sexual health, which certainly pushes many people's buttons, so I realized I had to develop a way to handle aggression or, simply, people who didn't agree with what I was saying. And sure enough, a while later I had a chance to practice. As part of a course on sexual health and outreach for people living on the street, I was asked to give a guest lecture to a group of fourth-year university students studying health-related disciplines such as social work, nursing, and so on. Not as intimidating as the physicians I had worked with, but still daunting. Little me was onstage in a big lecture hall at a prestigious university in the city I lived in. I had 150 faces looking at me expectantly. Once again, imposter syndrome was hitting hard, but I had been asked to be there to impart knowledge and wisdom they thought I had.

The presentation went well, but then came the question-and-answer period. One of the students stood up and proceeded to grill me on the research and practices. I remember thinking, "Oh, why me?" He asked, "Why should we be wasting our time with drug users and people living on the street?" He said he had *other* research that supported the opposite of what I was saying. This pushed a lot of buttons for me: it was exactly the kind of prejudice I'd been fighting against for years, and here was someone presenting it as unquestionable fact to undermine my efforts.

But by this point, I'd had more experience with this type of questioning. I also realized that there will always be someone who will disagree with me, and that's okay—I don't need to convince them. So I had practiced my response. The key is not to get angry or defensive, or to engage in an arguing match. I took a deep breath. Mentally, I took a step back (this is key! Sometimes I physically take a step back too—this helps me disconnect from the energy of having to argue and convince), and then I calmly said, "The information in this course is based on the research I shared earlier. If you have other information, I'd be more than happy to hear about it after the session."

Of course, 99 percent of the time, the person doesn't come up after the course to share their research or information with me. I've found that that's not usually the purpose of their question. But I can truthfully say that I like when people do approach me, because it's only fair. If I want the audience to be open to my information, I need to be open to theirs. Over the last twenty-five years, this has become my standard approach and response. The deep breath and mental step back allow me to get into the right mindset so I can respond in a way that maintains my integrity and authority in front of the audience while at the same time respecting the person who is asking the question, regardless of what their motivation is.

This is why it's important for you to find out what puts your back up about your topic. Do the mindset shift first. That step can't be avoided. Then develop a response that you can easily step into that feels right for you and that maintains your integrity and the integrity of the person asking the question.

Building BRIDGES

Now that you've analyzed your topic of change, let's create the structure through which to deliver it. I like to follow an acronym I've used many times and taught others: BRIDGES.

B: How will you create a bridge to your audience so you can relate to each other? Where are they at today? What are their issues with the change?

R: What is the rationale—why will this be worthwhile? What is its potential impact on society, customers, the company, the team, and the individual?

I: What are your intentions and objectives? How will you create dissatisfaction with the status quo while honoring the past? What is your aspiration for and vision of the future?

D: How will you do this—how will you achieve this goal?

G: What has been people's growth so far?

E: What are your expectations, and what do you commit to doing?

S: What is the summary—what are the top three takeaways that are most important for the audience to know or remember?

Here's an example:

Bridge: I know many of you may be nervous about how to get people to listen to your ideas so you can spark action and lead change that matters.

Rationale: Yet, I also know from years of practice that if you incorporate the material from this book into your repertoire, you will elevate your effectiveness and engage even more people so they take action on the ideas that are important to you.

Intention: The goal of this book is to help you understand yourself, gain insights on change and how to engage others, and learn a story structure for getting your ideas out in the world so people can take action on them. You're already good at this! Yes, you are. Or you wouldn't be driven to be even better. I also believe that you are effective at getting your ideas out there.

Do: If you incorporate the principles in this book and practice the activities, I know that you can reach your goal.

Growth: I know you can do this because you've made it this far in the book, and I also know, from my years of work, that people who pick up books like this and want to engage others to create change that matters have the solid foundation to do this.

Expectations: I truly expect you to get your amazing ideas out into the world to be heard so that, with others, you can effect change that matters, and I commit to guiding you through this process.

Summary: When you understand yourself deeply and learn how to engage others in change, and combine that with a solid structure for your message, people will hear your ideas and want to take action on them.

You may be thinking, "That was easy for him to write that." But I actually had to go back to the Intentions section when I got to Summary, as I realized I needed to fine-tune them. Be patient with yourself; it is an iterative process. And take note: You may need a few versions of your story: a five-minute one, a fifteen-minute one, even a thirty-minute one. But having taught this process for years, I can guarantee, with this structure, you'll have even more success with engaging others in your ideas. Once you have your ideas structured in BRIDGES, it's much easier to have the conversations to lead change.

At the end of her book, *It's Always Something*, comedian Gilda Radner said, "I wanted a perfect ending... Now I've learned, the hard way, that some poems don't rhyme, and some stories don't have a clear beginning, middle and end... Life... is about not knowing, having to change, taking the moment and making the best of it, without knowing what's going to happen next. Delicious ambiguity." As you lead change, you also need to be very comfortable in ambiguity. Once you have a structure, it's much easier to deviate from the plan and be in that "delicious ambiguity." Once we are in conversation, we have to be open to the ambiguity that comes with it.

Key Principles of a Story to Create Change

There are twelve more things I want you to know about creating a compelling change story to spark action in others. As you fine-tune your story, keep these key principles in mind:

1 **You can't change anyone.** You can't make anyone do anything. (Read those two sentences again!) However, you can create an environment conducive for people to change.

2 **Shift your mindset from "convince" to "educate and discuss."** Get others engaged in crafting the change story. You don't need to convince anyone of anything, which is very much a one-way process. You are not a salesperson! Take the pressure off. Isn't that a relief? Get into the educator mindset—a two-way process. You are here to create an environment of success.

3 **Create relatability.** Build the bridge with the audience before you do the reveal. Frame the topic or story.

4 **Incorporate rational and emotional elements.** Rational: How will this impact me? Will I have to increase my skills? Emotional: Will I want to work with this new team? Are we not doing well now? Combine information and data with what the story tells about the information.

5 **Bring people in gently if the topic can be perceived as difficult or challenging.** Don't hit people over the head to wake them up to your topic. That usually disengages them.

6   **Convey your own excitement.** Use phrases like "I feel..." and "I want us to do this because..." without letting your passion take you away. (This is one I've had to work on extensively; I can turn into a bulldozer if I get too excited about a topic, or get frustrated, which comes out as "Why can't you see this as I do?")

7   **Share examples.** Illustrating relevant examples will help you connect and resonate with your audience. Remember, the change happens in the mind of the other person.

8   **Find similarities of past successes.** When we remind people of the evidence or proof of their past successes, we remove doubt and give people the courage to step into the change.

9   **Be honest.** Don't sugarcoat. Don't put a positive spin on a bad situation. Sometimes you have to be in the negative to get out of it.

10 **Don't feel you have to have all the answers.** You don't! (Isn't it nice not to have that pressure as well?)

11 **Don't set yourself up as the "expert."** Share what makes you uncomfortable or unsure. Vulnerability builds trust.

12 **Move away from buzzwords.** Cliché terms such as "productivity" or "efficiency" can turn people off. Explain what the audience will actually experience or see differently.

I suggest reviewing these twelve points regularly to incorporate them into your mindset, as these points will impact how you decide to engage others in your ideas to create the change you want.

TALKING POINTS

- Get in the habit of analyzing your stories and how you tell them.

- Anchor information in people's heads and hearts.

- Create dissatisfaction with the status quo but honor the past.

- Understand your audience—deeply.

- Understand yourself—including what pushes your buttons.

- Build BRIDGES.

- You don't need to convince anyone of anything. Get into the educator mindset.

8

Choose Your Words Carefully

"If you want what you're saying heard, then take your time and say it so that the listener will actually hear it."

MAYA ANGELOU

NOW, LET'S ZOOM IN for a moment. We've been talking about the big picture of the story you want to tell and the right mindset to be in to deliver it— let's pause and look closely at the words. As a kid who talked a lot and now as an adult who makes a living speaking, I've learned through trial and error that when I use certain words to talk with others, people move closer and get engaged in what I'm saying, whereas certain other kinds of language unintentionally push people away or disconnect them from hearing me during times of change.

In an organizational setting, the words you use can motivate your team *or* discourage them. In a personal setting, it's exactly the same. Words can't change the reality of the situation, but they can alter how your colleagues *perceive* that reality, which has real implications for their work. Sometimes (quite often, actually), we need to really listen to our own stories for the kind of clarity, processing, healing, and perspective shifting that promotes positive action on the part of our listeners.

Here are what I've found to be the top twelve phrases *not* to use to spark action—and twelve phrases to use instead.

1. Don't say: "This will be easy."

Even if the people you are talking to recognize the need for change, it's never an easy process to go through. If you have people who are resisting change, the job becomes even harder.

In either case, telling people that change will be easy might be met with skepticism. Remember—you've had time to think about your ideas, but they are new to others, so your perspective of the process is a lot different from theirs. If you say the change will be easy, they may perceive your outlook as naive, misinformed, or disconnected from their concerns.

Do say: "It'll be a challenge, and we'll get through it."
The people you are trying to engage will appreciate your honesty and transparency about dealing with change, as well as your confidence that the pain will be only temporary. Be ready to provide support and listen to any issues that may come up.

2. Don't say: "Don't worry about it."

Very few things sound as dismissive as this phrase. The first thought running through their head might be,

"What makes you so confident?" Sure, we *hope* that everything will be fine, but frankly, who knows what problems will arise in the process, or what the end result might actually be? The longer and more complex the change you are asking them to bring to fruition, the less likely you will be able to predict the end result.

Do say: "Here's how we'll get through this idea/change/issue."
Map out how you will handle any risks and uncertainties that might arise. By getting the people around you involved, you'll be able to manage expectations as the plan is implemented. They'll feel more confident knowing you have a plan to deal with any issues that might come up.

3. Don't say: "You need to get on the train."

Or something to this effect. This will only result in shutting down further dialogue with your team. You'll risk sparking resentment in people whose resistance to change just got stronger. You might even convert some believers into non-believers!

The truth is that people don't *have* to get on any "train." Everyone has a choice. You could put the most innovative systems, supports, and measures in place, but the people you are talking with will ultimately decide for themselves whether they will engage in the change. Remember: we can't *make* people do anything. This is a hard principle for many of us to accept, including me— but it's true.

Do say: "I want to hear your concerns about this change/idea/ problem/solution."

When you show an honest interest in people's concerns about your idea, you demonstrate a willingness to engage with your workforce. This will also give you the opportunity to coach, support, and solve any problems that get brought up.

You may not be able to satisfy everyone's concerns, but your efforts will still be recognized and remembered by the people you are trying to engage.

4. Don't say: "These are all the positive reasons you should go along with this change."

"Positive" is relative. What's positive to you might not be positive to the people you are trying to engage. The change will be much harder if people think the impact on them or others will be negative.

Do say: "Here's why we're making this change, and this is the expected impact."

Openly discuss the positive and negative aspects and listen to and address any concerns. Providing a balanced approach builds trust and shows you aren't out of touch with the reality of the change—whether it's good or bad.

Remember: addressing the concern might not mean solving it, but the people you are engaging are more likely to be happy their thoughts were acknowledged.

5. Don't say: "Trust me."

Even if you have a long, trusting relationship with the people you are talking with, trust depends on much more. With a number of unknown variables that can happen during change, you'll need more than just relationship trust to get through the process of getting people to take action on your ideas.

The concept of trust is more complicated than trust in a single person or organization. Trust comes through action and information, not through a plea that might suggest you have something to hide.

Do say: "What can I do to help you manage the change?"

People want to know what's going to change, what's going to stay the same, what they still have control over, and what they won't. Trust alone won't answer those questions. Dialogue will.

Offer open, honest conversation about the change. Others will be more likely to develop trust in you and the change process ahead.

6. Don't say: "We are going to find efficiencies."

This is a scary one that sometimes gets translated as "job loss." This is what happens if you don't clearly state what you mean, how the change will affect people, and what the side effects might be.

We tend to use cushy words that are intended to soften the blow of what's really going on. Whether or not job losses are ahead, saying something like this will create a climate of fear, doubt, and uncertainty, which no one wants anywhere. And the resistance to change will become even stronger.

Do say: "Here are the inefficiencies we're looking to solve."
Be completely clear about what this means, identifying which inefficiencies the change will solve, as well as which efficiencies won't be affected. Most of the people I've worked with over the years appreciate candor, even if it's difficult to hear at first.

With honest, open communication, you'll be able to alleviate many of the doubts and concerns that arise with ideas that can seem very disruptive.

7. Don't say: "First world problems."

Sometimes when people tell us about their problems, we wonder why they are making such a big deal about such a seemingly small issue. The internet is slow; their microwave stopped working; they got a flat tire. "First world problems, Veronica!" you want to remind your complaining colleague. The trouble with this approach is that it negates the pressure of what that person is feeling at the moment. While in the grand scheme of things "first world problems" may be accurate, that response belittles their experience. (On a side note, for various reasons, we don't tend to classify regions as first, second, or third world anymore.)

Do say: "That really sounds like it was a hassle."
Or something else that recognizes how they are feeling in the moment. Acknowledging what is going on with someone at that moment and just putting yourself in their shoes keeps them engaged in the dialogue.

8. Don't say: "Everything will be all right."

When someone comes to you with worries about something they are facing, at work or in their personal life, you may want to reassure them—which is a good thing! However, simply telling them that it will be all right or that everything will work out minimizes the situation and may not even be accurate. It could be perceived as putting a positive spin on a bad situation, or as a simple platitude to keep them quiet. You don't know if it will be okay. Sometimes things don't work out. They are feeling the way they do because they are facing uncertainty about the future, and no matter what you say, your words can't change the reality of that uncertainty.

Do say: "Regardless of how this turns out..."
An approach like this one allows you to be in that uncertainty *with* them. To meet them where they are at. You recognize, with them, that none of us knows what the future holds. However, whatever happens, you do

know that you can support them: "Regardless of how this turns out, I'll be here for you" or "Regardless of how this turns out, I'll share the information with you." Whatever is relevant for the situation. The greatest gift you can give someone in the face of uncertainty is being with them no matter how the situation plays out.

9. Don't say: "At least ..."

It's often said that we teach what we most need to learn. While I don't believe that's true all the time, not long ago, it rang true for me. I heard myself saying, "At least you still have your job," to my friend Anita, who was describing a difficult work-related situation to me. I immediately apologized and asked Anita to continue her story.

When we respond in this manner, we are usually trying to put a positive spin on the situation. While trying to cheer them up and remind them of what they still have is well-intended, what they most *need* at the time is probably just to be heard and validated.

Do say: "It sounds like that was difficult."

Or something similar! Paraphrase what you've heard. The situation really just requires you to listen and acknowledge what is going on for the other person. You can best demonstrate you are listening by repeating what they have told you in your own words, which can also clarify your understanding. You may also try asking questions to understand more, or asking, "Is there any way I can help?" (as opposed to stating the solution *you* think they need).

10. Don't say: "Can we ...?"

If there's one thing that's inspired me during the last few years, it's seeing how individuals, organizations, and businesses have developed innovative ways to deliver their services. They didn't do it by saying, "Can we ...?"

When you ask a question such as "Can we do this?" the answer is simply "yes" or "no." This close-ended response does not give you the information you need to expand your thinking and be innovative in your approach.

Do say: "How can we ...?"

"How can we ...?" moves you to a solution-focused approach and expands your thinking to develop and create new ways of doing what you need to do. Influencing change works best with open-ended questions, such as "How can we make this happen?" This leads to innovative possibilities and group solutions that are often better thought-out and more likely to succeed than solutions devised in isolation. It's when you ask, "How can we ...?" instead of "Can we ...?" that you get unstuck during change and create purposeful action.

11. Don't say: "You should ..."

When you use the word "should" with others (or with yourself: "I should've done this"), it creates blame, guilt, and sometimes even shame. It also takes away the concept of choice. Everyone has a choice. You can choose not to do something the right way. There are consequences of that choice.

I'm not saying to ignore the "right" way of doing certain things. What I'm saying is, when you use "should" to influence someone to change their behavior, it will disengage them from listening to you.

I caught myself doing this with my property developer (and real estate agent), Michelle, when building a new house. Due to the complexity of the land we live on—conservation land—there are several hoops to jump through. I caught myself saying, "I should've checked this out more in-depth."

I immediately thought, "Darn—I actually said 'should'! I could've said that differently!" And had a little chuckle. And Michelle said, "Shoulda, woulda, coulda. Let's figure out what to do!" Her saying that knocked me out of feeling bad about a decision I had made and pointed me in the right direction, so we could actually take action on change that matters to me.

You can do something incorrectly and change it without making yourself "bad" or "stupid" (or insert your own word here that you beat yourself up with) or making someone else "wrong."

Do say: "I'd suggest . . ." or "You could . . ."

"You should do it this way" becomes "Next time, you could do it this way." Or "Next time, I'd suggest you involve these people sooner." Or "The regulations say to do it this way." This approach keeps people open and more receptive to your ideas and to changing their behavior.

When it comes to engaging others in your ideas to take action, erase the word "should" from your vocabulary. This helps you guide people down the path of change that matters.

12. Don't say: "This is lousy." (You can insert your own negative word here! Terrible, awful, gloomy.)

Negative emotions creep into our language all the time. "This is a lousy report." "This is a yucky day." "This is terrible work." "This was a disastrous evening." The problem with this language is that it puts a blanket negative comment over the entire situation. When you layer in negative emotion, it clouds the facts.

"But, but, but—what if someone dies, what if I get laid off, what if I get sick?" you may be saying. If a terrible life event happens—whether regarding health, career, or family—by all means use negative language. I'm the first person to say don't put a positive spin on a really bad situation. If it's bad, sit with it. It's not always appropriate to "fix" things right away when bad things happen.

Do say: "This can be improved."

When you are trying to engage others in your ideas to take action, although you may have an initial emotional reaction to something, it is important that your words skip the emotion and focus on the facts. For the examples above, you could say instead: "This report has a few errors." "It's a wet day." "This work needs to improve."

"This evening could have been better." Removing emotion from your vocabulary in these examples gives people an opportunity to listen and stay engaged without having to counter you with an equally powerful emotional response. Heightened emotion disengages people from your proposal and makes them harder to connect with. Conversely, presenting them with facts gives them something they can work with.

Sparking action in others requires a shift from how we may normally communicate in situations. When you practice removing from your vocabulary the types of negative phrases I've given above and then substituting the suggestions, you will notice how people stay engaged in your conversations differently.

From the examples I've provided, you can see how our normal responses often halt others' ability to engage in change rather than facilitate it. Just in case you don't believe me, when people use the above sayings on you, whether the ones to say or not say, gauge your reaction! Which ones leave you open to change and which ones not so much? Try out the suggestions above to see what works. I think you will find you are more likely to be heard and to be able to instigate the change that matters to you with the new phrases.

TALKING POINTS

- Don't be dismissive (even if you think the issues are silly)—take people's concerns seriously and address them.

- Listen, and make sure they know you are listening.

- Don't ignore the downside, but don't wallow in it.

- Pay attention to emotions—yours and theirs.

- Use the right language to keep people moving down the path of change.

9

Go Deeper: Tell the Whole Story

*"Out beyond ideas of wrongdoing and rightdoing, /
there is a field. I'll meet you there."*

RUMI

ABOUT TWENTY YEARS AGO, I was paragliding in the mountains of the Czech Republic. On one unfortunate day, I made a bad landing and shattered the lower part of my left leg. I flew back to Vancouver, BC, where I was living at the time, underwent surgery, and prepared myself to rebuild the strength in my leg.

As part of the recovery, the surgeon advised me to go swimming three times per week. Sounds great, right? That's what I thought when he told me.

Boy, was I wrong. From day one, the reality of the nuances and intricacies of the recovery process became painfully evident. How was I supposed to get from my home to a pool at least eight blocks away on a set of crutches? How could I get a bathing suit over a huge, swollen leg I couldn't bend, and then get from the changing room to the pool on one leg? And after I was done in the pool, how would I get out?

Without the support and guidance I needed, my recovery didn't go as planned. However, what I learned was that tasks can seem easy on the surface, but once you get into the details of it from the end user's point of view, the intricacies can seem insurmountable. Which they did. So I actually never went swimming.

What ended up really helping me in my recovery was this patient, helpful physiotherapist I worked with for a year. She truly understood how to break down large changes into manageable tasks—things I needed to do like using crutches, figuring out how to get up and down stairs, and other activities essential to my recovery. (She also offered to help me with the swimming task, but I felt like that was out of reach at that point.) After one year, with her guidance and skilled support, I was able to learn how to walk again. How great is that!

As you may guess, the key lesson here is this: just telling someone to do something because of the benefits, no matter how well-intentioned or kind-hearted, doesn't generally work when the person you are talking to has a lot on their plate. The surgeon wasn't intentionally telling me to do something I felt was out of reach. He was telling me what he thought was best!

We can apply this lesson to your current position as a change leader: although change might appear daunting, with help, guidance, and determination to face the challenge head-on, you can lead people toward achieving the changes you want.

It's Not All Benefits

People who are passionate about an idea often focus on selling people on the benefits of their idea rather than engaging others in the actions of change. This is largely because we live in an advertising-driven society, where product benefits are continuously hurled at us in an everlasting sales pitch on TV, online, and in print. We've become conditioned to give and receive information in this way.

But "benefits, benefits, benefits" doesn't get people to listen to you in the real world. I often see proof of this in corporate settings, where someone proposes a new idea and says, "Here are the benefits to the organization," and people respond, "That's really great, but it's going to create more work for me," or "That sounds nice, but we could lose our jobs with this merger," or "I appreciate that you want us to update and change our language here, but we've been using it for forty years, so how is this not just about being politically correct?" When you ignore impact, the people you're talking to will think that you're completely out of touch with reality.

In many cases, we try tuning in to the WIIFM ("What's In It For Me?") radio station to get others on board, emphasizing the other person's direct personal gains. While that is good in that we want to get into the heads of the people we are trying to engage, it can become a challenge if there really isn't much "in it" for the other person individually. In certain contexts of workplace change, some people can be motivated by the promise of such "carrots" as streamlined systems, better efficiencies, and reduced waste down the road, but many of us—including me—are often more concerned about how the change will affect them in the short term.

Always remember that although the benefits of change might not exist for the people you work with, the immediate impact *will* exist.

So, you have to be willing to articulate the possible negative impacts as well as the benefits: "If we do this, more people will be helped, though it's going to require extra time from us, and it's going to make us feel awkward and weird." When you paint the picture of how it's going to look warts and all, and do so with the promise or implication that you're all in it together and will get through it, the outcome changes because there is empathy.

This is why we can't just listen to WIIFM—we need the more comprehensive WIOM ("What's the Impact On Me?"). The WIOM principle focuses on the reality that people need to be told the actual, tangible, short-term effects of the change (or your ideas or whatever you are trying to engage them in) and be given the support and information they need to help them through the transition.

WIIFM Versus WIOM

You're probably used to using WIIFM rather than WIOM in your own lifestyle decisions. For example, let's say you find a beautiful new house and are considering purchasing it. First, you consider some of the WIIFMs:

• Bigger space for family and friends

• A neighborhood that better suits your needs

- A fresh, exciting new start for you and your family

- New friends and contacts

- A feeling of control over your decisions

  Then you look at the WIOMs:

- Higher property taxes

- Increased mortgage payments

- Uprooting your family into a new, unfamiliar space

- Time spent packing and unpacking

- Moving time and costs

You most likely won't decide to take action until you examine the benefits *and* the impact—both positive and negative.

These two lists of lifestyle changes parallel those in the workplace. You feel the effect of some of the WIOMs right away, and reap the benefits from the WIIFMs over a longer period of time. By balancing the two, you decide whether the move is a good one for you and your family. But in the home-buying scenario, you at least have some control over the decision-making. In the workplace, you might not, even if the WIIFM list is much longer than WIOM.

Here are a few short-term concerns that people involved in workplace change might have:

- **Loss of job or position:** Even if your colleagues truly have nothing to fear, this will be creeping in the back of their minds. Will I be replaced or transitioned into something uncomfortable and unfamiliar? Or could this change put me out of a job?

- **Fear of change:** Your colleagues have been doing the same thing in the same manner using the same equipment and software for years. These tools are predictable and they have worked up until now. How long will it take for them to understand and embrace a new, unknown system, if they're even able to?

- **Loss of routine:** People love routine. It gives them a sense of control over their workday. The idea of change can take that sense of control away, leaving your coworkers confused and uncertain. Can they unlearn one routine and adopt a new one with minimal interruption to productivity?

- **Loss of face:** No one wants to lose face in front of a manager, much less in front of a client. Your colleagues know the current system inside out and can answer client questions with authority. But will they feel slow and awkward answering client questions when using the new system?

- **Peer pressure:** Embracing change is harder for some than for others. Your colleagues might worry that their coworkers will be able to transition faster than they can, possibly affecting their morale and creating workplace tension that might not have been there before.

In the workplace, you may be tempted to take a higher philosophical viewpoint—"something good will come of this"—but your colleagues might not appreciate this approach. With mortgages to pay, kids in university, and other financial obligations, your colleagues will be more concerned about how the change will affect them right now and in the near future. Even if the changes are good for everyone involved, people may not immediately embrace them until they see the results for themselves.

In fact, I've found it's better not to lead with the benefits and WIIFM but rather end with them so the people I'm talking to know I understand their perspective. It's also good to end on a positive note. People who feel heard tend to get on board! You want them to think, "Wow, they're thinking about things from my point of view," because, remember, the change, the impact, the influence—all of that stuff happens in the other person's mind. Tell them how to integrate this into their lives. How to make it work for them. How is it all going to work, from their point of view?

That's the key to creating impact—and getting change to happen. Your plan to involve others in your ideas to create change needs to provide clear, open-door, transparent communication to ensure the smoothest change possible. There will always be resistance, but when you're trying to engage others, the dialogue just doesn't stop; rather, you can look at how you can provide support to the people you are working with. Honesty mixed with diplomacy is crucial as well, even if it causes a bit of concern. My experience is, people appreciate hard truths over falsehoods, indifference, or silence. Remember this one guideline: while there isn't always a WIIFM, there is always a WIOM.

Meet in the Field

Over the last thirty years of working with diverse groups of people in many different environments, I've discovered that there is one thing we have in common in order to thrive: the power to break through limitations and create positive change in our world.

As Rumi, the thirteenth-century Sufi poet and mystic, put it, "Out beyond ideas of wrongdoing and rightdoing, / there is a field. I'll meet you there." This quote perfectly summarizes my philosophy. If you want to get others to engage in your ideas, you must meet in the field Rumi refers to. This involves suspending judgment about what you feel is right or wrong about the change you're facing, and developing a strategy to bring skeptical people on board.

If you do the above, you can get into the right mindset, which is about anticipating and seizing the opportunity that change provides.

Whether you are a community organizer, a budding entrepreneur, or a leader in your organization, you know that change cannot be executed successfully without the support of the people or groups you are working with. This means you have to see the change from their viewpoints and show them how to overcome the issues—both positive and negative.

TALKING POINTS

- It's not all benefits, so don't pretend it is.

- For every WIIFM, there's a WIOM. Make sure you address all the impacts of the proposed change.

- Don't impose value judgments on a change or on people's responses to it.

10

Build a Bridge
with Hot Topics

---

*"Being in your head is all about worrying how other
people see you. Let your real self come out."*

RUPAUL

WAS WORKING with a speaker—I'll call her Chelsea—
who really wanted to create change that matters. She
used to get onstage in front of a professional audience
and start out with the fact that she'd had a drug addiction in the past. That's a heavy topic to open with, and
the audience disengaged from her after hearing that.
Many people couldn't relate, and others may have found
it triggering. What she was speaking on wasn't drug use
but leadership, and when you get into it, her story is
funny and relatable, but by that point, people couldn't
hear it.

So I worked with her to craft her story so she could
bring people in easily. We talked about anticipating
objections, for example, "I don't have a drug addiction,
so I'm not going to listen to you" or "That would never
be me." And then we discussed how we could create
relatability.

Everyone overdoes something. *Everyone*. (I can eat a
whole bag of chocolate chip cookies—I can relate!) So,
onstage, Chelsea began her new talk like this: "So I'm
sure there are probably some of you in the audience who

really like to eat a lot of cookies and put your hand in that cookie jar. You don't need to put up your hand, but I know there's a bunch who do." And then she continued, drawing them in further: "I'm sure some of you really like to get into shopping and sometimes you might shop a little too much. Some of you like cigarettes. Some of you might gossip a lot. Some of you just can't stop with that one chip out of the big bag. All of us have things we like to do a lot and often end up overdoing. And every one of you has something, don't you?" Everybody nodded their heads and smiled and laughed. And then she said, "Well, you know, I really liked to do something a lot too ... that white powder you pop up your nose. I used to do a lot of that. And I know that all of you can relate because you all like to do cookies, chips, and other stuff sometimes a bit too much." The audience was still nodding; some were maybe a bit shocked, but they were in the palm of her hand at that point.

Everybody was brought in on the same perspective and could relate to her. That is the key part when you're talking about loaded topics: create the relatability first, and then time your reveal of the loaded topic—and then after you've revealed it, show your similarities again. Help them feel connected—all of them.

We're getting into the harder topics, the ones people have judgments about before we even utter a word. But let's admit that in today's world, just about any subject is tricky. Everything these days can feel like a hot-button issue; so many things have become polarizing. There are minefields everywhere, so whether you are trying to create change in diversity or sales leadership, you are going to run into areas that have the potential to alienate or offend people in your audience.

The insights shared in this chapter will help you build a bridge that will allow you to better connect with the people you're talking to. And *all* of us who want to create change have to build that bridge, no matter what our topic is. All of us are trying to create change on the planet, or you wouldn't be reading this book.

Jumping headfirst into the tricky topic right at the beginning is usually not the best approach. Even if people know you are there to speak on that topic and are sitting in their seats looking at you expectantly, *they aren't ready yet.* You need to establish rapport and help them feel comfortable—both with the topic in general and with you as the teacher. This is what the bridge does.

You also need to be ready, by the way. Your stories are important and deserve to be heard, but they also need to be healed inside you before they can come out, and this means that not all stories are ready to be told. Stories about advocacy for the marginalized or about addiction and recovery can be difficult for people for various reasons. These are frankly easy for many people to disconnect from, despite seeming inspirational on the surface. This is why knowing yourself first matters so much.

Don't Push

A number of years ago, I was on the hunt for a new car. I knew exactly what type of car I wanted and how much I wanted to spend. On a Friday, I walked into the dealership where I wanted to get my car.

The salesperson came up to me and asked me what I wanted. I pointed to the exact car. Not the highest priced, but a mid-range model that had all the features I required. The salesperson launched into a one-way stream of benefits of higher-priced cars: "What about this one over here? This one has a better stereo system." But I wanted that one there—I pointed again. "But this one here has way more benefits," the salesperson said, "like larger engine, better on the road, larger trunk."

Now, I expect a salesperson to try to upsell, but after a few times, just give me the car I want. After about ten minutes of back-and-forth, I could see he didn't know how to engage with a customer, so I thanked him for his time and I walked out, frustrated.

However, there was another dealership nearby that had a similar category of car. Different brand, but close enough for me. I went in. Met the salesperson, Jim. Jim asked me what type of car I was looking for. I said, four doors, good on gas, sunroof, good-sized trunk, and comfortable for a tall person. Jim then asked, "Why do you want a car like that?" I told him that I do a lot of driving; I have to drive back and forth from the city to the cottage as well as to client sites for speaking engagements or workshops. "What's your budget?" he asked. I told him. "Want to test drive a few?" Sure! Within twenty minutes, I'd signed the deal. I still negotiated the price. He upsold me on one item—which I agreed I needed.

After we'd signed, I said to Jim, "You are an amazing salesperson. Do you teach this to people?" He said,

"Thank you. My goal is to really find out what the customer needs and provide that for them. The only way I know how to do that is to listen and ask questions, and then we can work together to find the best car. You are more likely to work with me again if we do that together."

I still go to that dealership all these years later, even though Jim isn't there anymore. They still hire the best people, and I trust their guidance from service through to sales—whether it's Ishmil, Jamie, or Dana. How many people can say that?

Now *that's* building a bridge with a lasting impact.

When you are trying to spark action in others and you are under pressure to perform, you can unintentionally become like the first salesperson I dealt with. However, if you remember to build a bridge first, I can guarantee you will have greater success in getting people to take action on your ideas.

As I've mentioned before, the bridge is a two-way process, not a one-way, didactic information drop. The bridge includes everything you say, from when you first open your mouth at a meeting—or in my case, onstage— to when you finally dive into the meat of your content. That bridge will help you walk the people you are talking to from where they are right now safely over to your topic so they can feel comfortable enough to listen with open ears and minds.

Again, the words also matter, especially on loaded topics or any topic that can be interpreted in different ways. Examine the language you use and consider it carefully, because your beliefs may not be those of other people. I'm not saying to water down your message, just that you need to bring people in gently so they can hear you; otherwise, they won't. Anticipate objections and reactions. In the example we started with, when Chelsea used the word "addiction," it was a loaded word with different meanings for different people. If she was going to use it at all, she had to step gently up to it: "You know, I used to do a lot of putting the white powder up my nose. Some people might call it addiction. Some people might call it a problem. For me, it was an issue."

Another speaker I worked with—I'll call him Jesse—focused on diversity and inclusion conversations. An audience member mentioned a word they used. Jesse said, "That's transphobic. You shouldn't use that word." The audience member immediately shut down.

I talked to Jesse after and reminded him that while we may have a valid gut reaction to a word, some people are still learning and may use racist, homophobic, and transphobic terms that they don't intend as phobic, and if we want to bring people into our story about adopting change, we'll want to soften our own language so we can be heard by them and positively received. Applying labels to people pushes them away, which of course is the opposite of our goal. We may do it unintentionally—I can tell you that Jesse was not intentionally labeling that person—but the person took it that way. I suggested he rephrase it as, "People can interpret that as being transphobic." In this context, the language used by Jesse created a safe space for that person and other people to bring up other words they're using so they can learn without losing face.

Adjusting Your Style to Be Heard

You will have a range of people you engage with, and 50 percent or more will not hear you or take action if you follow only your own communication style. We need to understand our own style to be able to adjust how we communicate depending on our audience. You can't change everyone, but you can be heard, and you can create the space for others to engage in change. People are always free to choose, but they're not free from the consequences of their choices. Your job is to inform them of their choices so they can make the best ones on their own. If you don't understand how you and others send and receive information differently, I suggest taking a simple personality-type assessment such as the DiSC (Dominance, Influence, Steadiness, and Compliance) test, which you can find online. (There are many types of assessment tools out there. I like this one because it's simple and easy to apply. Just remember, this is a framework to understand differences, not a tool to label people.)

How do you know you are creating an impact? Listen and watch for nonverbal signs, "aha" moments, and other forms of engagement that show they are getting what you want them to get. Use your gut and innate ability to reframe and adjust so your audience can best hear your story.

At the beginning of our entrepreneurial careers, we often feel we have to appeal to everyone to get our voices heard. No, you most definitely don't. What you need is more of the *right* people who can hear you, and you get these only from speaking about your work in your own authentic, powerful voice. I have a client who used to work as a vice president of a large foundation; now, she is a coach for "marvelous mavens and women who want to shake up the world." You know instantly whether you want to work with her or not!

Using your voice to tell your story virtually or in person in a way that connects to others also helps you find the right group to make things happen exponentially. Gail Larsen, one of my teachers and mentors, says, "Work with people who can hear you, not with people who can't." Gail doesn't mean not using your voice to be heard. She means that when we structure our message to be heard, even when we have difficult topics, we create more change than if we focus our energy on someone or a group that just plain can't hear us. Make sure your message is clear and effective, and expect that there will always be some who won't hear it, so stop striving when it is clear who they are. It's not worth it to bang your head against a door that won't open.

When you put your real self out there and help others reach their full potential, it makes their life better as well as yours. My philosophy is: If you're doing well, I'm doing well, and now we can both do great work on the planet.

Anticipate Objections—or, Teaching Sex to Nuns

One of the stories I love to share in my workshops is about the time when I was teaching sex to nuns. Yes, it's a true story.

I have to tell you, these sisters were like *The Sound of Music* nuns. These were women who just wanted to do good on the planet. They did not want to convert people to Catholicism; they just wanted to provide services and resources to people who were living in the Downtown Eastside of Vancouver, which is often referred to as the poorest postal code in Canada. They were going to be working with sex workers. They were going to be working with injection drug users. They were going to be working with people who really were living right on the street. And they wanted to work with these people in a non-judgmental way.

It was the afternoon of day two of the workshop. The topic of sex wasn't something that could be covered early on because we had to create the safety to do it. And they knew we were going to cover it. So there we were, twenty-five nuns and I standing around in a circle, each with markers in hand, and on the floor were twenty-five pieces of flip chart paper. At the top of each paper was one word, and the word corresponded to a body part and the practices that went on with those body parts between the neck and the knees. (I'm sure you can guess what part body parts we are referring to!) I said, "On these pieces of paper, you'll notice body parts between the neck and the knees, and the practices that might go along with those body parts. Write down all the street terms, slang, swear words, words you heard as a kid in the schoolyard— all the 'dirty' words, any words that you can think of that describe those body parts or those practices that go along with the body parts."

They looked at me with big, wide eyes and were very nervous. So I took the first step and under one of the headings wrote a funny little word I'd heard in the school-yard when I was a kid. They all giggled. And then one of the nuns tiptoed out and wrote down another word. And then a few others wrote other words. Some sisters were laughing and giggling. And before you knew it, after ten minutes, the pages were full of slang, swear words, and street terms, and the sisters were silently reading them. And I tell you, there were some I'd never heard before, but these sisters had heard a lot of them, just like all of us who aren't Catholic nuns.

As we took a step back to analyze the words, we realized that the power was in the words and the language, and that the nuns could be desensitized to that. What that means is when someone who was living on the street came up to them and said, "Something's wrong with my [street word]," the Catholic sister didn't say, "Now, dear, it's called '[polite word].'" The sister was able to respond in a non-judgmental way about what was going on "down there." She didn't need to use the word, but she needed to not be shocked when she was hearing it.

As a result of learning about sexual health and how different people talked about different body parts, and having fun analyzing the language, the sisters were able to serve a whole new population of people they hadn't served before. How great is that? That's creating change that matters! These sisters had not been accustomed to working with people who were living in the Downtown Eastside, but with the appropriate language and approach, they were able to serve this marginalized group of people in a non-judgmental way. And I think they're still doing it today, thirty years later.

What I learned early on in my career, and I still see it today, is that self-imposed limitations are the greatest barrier to change. If these nuns could break through their limitations and do that activity in a group and serve a whole new population of people, I'm sure those of us *not* in that situation can learn to get our difficult ideas across to others so they can take action. I'm sure that in the workplace, we can get others to act on complex initiatives. I'm sure that when we want people to talk differently about other people, we can get them to use different language. And see the world through a totally new lens.

TALKING POINTS

- To ease people into hot topics, first find points of connection.

- Everyone can relate to a difficult topic. Find out how.

- You're not a salesperson. You're a bridge builder.

- Anticipate objections; don't push people away, bring people in.

- Work with people who can hear you.

- Self-imposed limitations are the greatest barrier to change.

11

Get Past "No"

---

*"I don't have a short temper. I just have
a quick reaction to bullshit."*

ELIZABETH TAYLOR

A S I'VE SAID throughout this book, when we want to spark action in others, even good change can be hard and have initial negative impacts on the people around us. And aversion to change is human nature and perfectly normal.

This is a truth of human nature: Whether we are business owners, community organizers, leaders, coaches, teachers, or parents—regardless of what role we are in—there are things we do that will tick others off and make them shut down. These kinds of disconnects usually happen when we're in conversations with others. We each have a communication style and pattern. And though we may think that we are doing the best job communicating with others, using all our bells and whistles and tricks and tools of the trade, it still seems as though some people can't hear us. But if they can't hear us, how are they supposed to take action on our ideas?

It happens in the other direction too. We're working and talking with someone and they're telling us information that is unintentionally pushing our buttons, or they're doing things that make us want to pull our hair out or internally scream. We're not able to get our voices heard then, either, because these people can't hear us and we can't hear them. It can lead to a total shutdown.

If you can't get your voice heard in a way that is respectful, it may be because you are unintentionally having a negative conversation. This can happen particularly when you are under great pressure during times of extreme change. When we are under stress and pressure, as mentioned earlier in the book, we can become very reactive. Whether it's being questioned or not agreeing with what the other person is saying, we can become defensive and shut down the conversation, especially when what we are asking really matters to us.

As mentioned earlier, the ability to be heard and spark action in others depends on how you adapt your approach so the other person can hear and take action—sometimes we need to dial up certain behaviors and dial some down. For example, because I'm such a raging extrovert and process my ideas verbally, I need to dial down my talking and dial up my ability to create space and silence so I can allow the other person to speak. You need to know what you're really great at in terms of how you communicate—how you use language and what words you use, in your tone and your voice, your nonverbal signals—to get a real understanding of who you are and where your strengths are in that way.

A Shocking Truth

But—sorry to say it again—there will always (or almost always) be naysayers. They'll pipe up and tell you all the ways in which your idea *can't* be done and why you shouldn't do it. They'll try to get you to stop with your passionate call to change. They will encourage you to allow your ideas to die before they even get a chance to be heard.

And sometimes *we* will be the naysayers. I know I've been the naysayer at times—the guy who said, "I've been here eleven years, so trust me, it can't be done."

But remember: no one brings up ideas in meetings that they think are silly. There is always a nugget of goodness in your ideas or other people's ideas. So stop and ask, "What's good about this idea?"

Here is an example I use in sessions that you can try now to see how easy or difficult it is for you to look for good in a potentially wild idea. Let's pretend we're in a meeting with a group of colleagues, and we are all coming together to determine how to make our organization more change-ready. I put up my hand and suggest that we give everyone electroshock therapy to make them ready to handle all the upcoming challenges.

Of course, you—along with everyone else—say, "Wait a minute, Gregg—that's illegal! What a terrible idea!" But I'll remind you that I am not a person who brings up ideas I think won't work. So, what's good about this idea? Make a list on a piece of paper! Try it.

What did you come up with? Perhaps things like: It's easy to schedule; it's one-size-fits-all; it weeds out the uncommitted. It's portable, groundbreaking, and innovative. It energizes people and resets them to be aligned as a team. It's efficient and easy to repeat; it focuses people.

The list could go on. When I'm with an in-person group, we can fill three flip chart pages—once people get unstuck from why this is a bad idea.

Now considering our list (and you can review the list you just made), we would not find one CEO on the planet who would *not* want us to come up with a way to make our organization change-ready that's easy to schedule, efficient, and weeds out the uncommitted. We want an idea that energizes people, aligns people as a team, focuses people, and so on. Who wouldn't want that?

So while electroshock therapy itself obviously won't work, we've elevated the conversation in just a few minutes by answering the question, "What's good in this idea?" We now have twenty or so criteria that can change the conversation. Instead of just randomly throwing ideas out as a group, let's now talk about ideas that fit some of these criteria that were in my rather disruptive (and, honestly, illegal) idea.

When I do this live with an audience, you can see the light bulbs go on. I remind them that if they'd shut down this idea as they had wanted to before, we would never have gotten here and we'd still be throwing random ideas around instead of having a more focused conversation that meets these twenty or so criteria.

Different Reasons for Resistance

You all know the reasons that people resist change. So I'm not going to go into them too deeply, as they've been covered extensively in many other people's works.

There's a natural level of skepticism that kicks in for a lot of people when they encounter ideas that may seem disruptive to them. It's not true for everyone; however, knowing this when you want to engage others in your ideas is critical because all they may need in order to get on board is more information or to have their questions answered.

I'm normally a very optimistic person; I see the good, and I'm very open to different things that occur. And yet, some years ago, my boss at the time said to me, "Why do you say no to every new idea that comes up? And then thirty minutes later, you go around to a yes."

I learned that I do tend to say no when someone's idea comes up that I don't agree with or I initially dislike. It's a quick reaction and I've had to learn how to manage that—to stop myself and ask, "What's good about this idea?" as we did above. (I'm still learning this lesson and practicing it!)

What do you do if you need to address an entire group of people with differing viewpoints? That, to be honest, is going to be your most common scenario. If you must address a whole group of diverse people, how do you engage them all?

You focus on four or five common themes that are important to the different groups of people present and make sure to address them so that people don't feel left out. It's not about speaking to the lowest common denominator; it's about finding what the themes are for each different group and making sure you address those in some capacity. It's definitely *not* about putting on the positive spin, either; it's more about the big-picture view and talking about the overall impact. As I've said, when we talk about impact, we want to be up front about any extra work required and the potential pain points involved in the change, and we need to do this while not overwhelming people with data.

As mentioned earlier, your job is to educate people and get them on board. You don't need to sell anyone on anything. It's not all "win friends and influence people" because, to be honest, that's impossible, especially during times of great change. Your role is to spark action by creating an environment for them in which to engage in your ideas—so they can take action on the change you are proposing.

Keep the Amygdala Out of It

The most important thing is to keep the amygdala out of it. Remember the amygdala, from chapter 2—the set of neurons in our brains that helps regulate emotions? According to Sunnie Giles, an expert on leadership and radical innovation, the number one job of leaders is to manage their team's emotional brains by avoiding triggering the amygdala, which would result in a fight-or-flight response. In other words, leaders are responsible for what's called "psychological safety."

Once the amygdala is involved, it's hard to be rational anymore. This is because when our emotional response gets triggered, our functioning cognitive brains become flooded with cortisol and other chemicals, resulting in a loss of working memory. We stop thinking clearly. That's why some people frequently get flustered when they get up in front of a group of people and feel pressured.

And it takes time for it to clear up. I remember being in a meeting with my boss at the time, a mathematician by training, who kept grilling me about my budget. After about ten minutes, I got completely tongue-tied and said I had to use the restroom. I left the room, and as I took a little walk, I became less flustered—meaning the cortisol and other chemicals were draining out of my brain. I walked back into the meeting calmly to answer the questions.

What's worse is that one person's amygdala response can set off another person's. If you've ever had a disagreement or verbal altercation with someone at home, you know this well. The conversation starts off fact-based: "Can you clean up all your toothpaste drips?" Then the other person responds, "How about when you get your dishes out of the sink?!" Before long, the cortisol, adrenaline, and other hormones and chemicals have kicked in, and all of a sudden, you're having a very different, very heated conversation. Things come out of your mouth and you have no idea where they came from.

Eventually, the disagreement breaks up somehow. You leave the room. The cortisol drains out of your brain.

Adrenaline cools down. Then you think, "I can't believe I said all that!" Then you may go back and apologize—as I have had to do many times.

This doesn't mean you need to be an expert in psychology or neuroscience to succeed in getting your ideas for change across. It only means you need to recognize these emotional activators and know what you can do to manage them, such as:

- Rigorously manage expectations—people want to predict the future as best they can. Help them do that.

- Be clear with your colleagues or people working with you about which tasks and processes people have control over and input on, and which ones they don't.

- Be honest and open about what will change and what will stay the same. We all like to be in our comfort zone, as that's where we are most productive. We are using the least amount of energy to do the maximum amount of work. But growth doesn't happen there!

- Create an inclusive change environment—whether it's a meeting, a Zoom call, or a one-on-one—so no one feels left out. Feeling like an outsider doesn't generally contribute to productive teamwork. With technology, you can do this with people who are scattered geographically all over the place.

- Face the negative aspects of change head-on to avoid creating an atmosphere of false positivity.

While there are a lot of great models, frameworks, and theories out there, I don't believe there is a single "right" approach to change. In fact, there are a lot of different approaches that need to be tailored to each situation depending on the environment, people, and type of change required.

Using this information, we can go back to the questions we had at the beginning of the book: What is the new story you want to create for yourself, your community, your organization, and the planet? What do you want to spark action on to lead change that matters?

TALKING POINTS

- Watch out for things you do and ways you say things that make people shut down.

- There will always be naysayers.

- Don't reject someone's idea out of hand; look for what's good in it. There is always a nugget to be found.

- People have different reasons for resisting change, and none of them should be ignored.

- Do your best to keep the amygdala uninvolved!

12

Make Change That Sticks

*"There's no use trying," [Alice] said.
"One can't believe impossible things."
"I daresay you haven't had much practice," said the Queen.
"When I was your age, I always did it for
half-an-hour a day. Why, sometimes I've believed
as many as six impossible things before breakfast."*

LEWIS CARROLL, *Through the Looking-Glass*

CHANCES ARE, someone you know has broken a New Year's resolution—not just once but every year. Sometimes, it seems we make them with the expectation of breaking them! But we certainly don't mean to fall short of our goals. When we make these annual resolutions, we truly do it with the best intentions of seeing them through. However, we often fail because we haven't thought through the issues we are facing and the challenges to implement the resolutions, or put the appropriate supports in place to help us move forward.

The same can be applied to any type of change you want to make happen—say, in community building or in your business or organization. You need to combine the right elements to not only get through the change process successfully but also make the change stick long term. I frame both these ideas as two equations that can easily be used whenever you want to lead others down the path of change you want.

Positive Action Equation:
Getting Through Change Successfully

Knowledge and wisdom are important to have in leadership, especially when you are trying to make others receptive to the change you propose. However, to be effective, you also need them to implement the change successfully. This sounds simple, but I find it's often overlooked. This idea forms the basis for what I call the Positive Action Equation:

Wisdom + Action = Change

Most of us gain knowledge or wisdom from our own experiences: at an event, searching the internet, reading an article or book, talking with colleagues, through our own life experiences, or from any number of other ways. As has been said, knowledge is power, but knowledge on its own is meaningless. One must act on it.

For example, you might go to a conference, take notes, and meet with dozens of people to gain the knowledge you need to help your organization reach its goals. However, if you go back to the office and don't apply the insights, what good does the knowledge do?

I find that many people who want to engage others in their ideas start the change process the same way I would—they talk to colleagues, read books and articles, and meet with their manager. However, many of them haven't yet taken steps to actually move the change forward. In other words, they have gleaned the wisdom they need, but there comes a point when you have to stop gathering information and take small, simple, and manageable steps to get your ideas going. This is what I refer to as the "action" step.

Especially in cases where change is more complex, we may not be sure which steps to take first. Any step forward is better than no step at all (most of the time!), so start small and see what happens. You can always backtrack and try something else. Waiting until you feel it's 100 percent safe to proceed may leave you feeling paralyzed because change can be dynamic and involve many variables. You might never feel 100 percent about every step, so don't procrastinate—take the risk of that first small step. As you move forward, you'll start taking additional steps with more confidence. Also, it's equally important to try to take these steps as part of a plan or a process so you aren't feeling like you are randomly throwing spaghetti against the wall, hoping a piece sticks!

One thing I've noticed working with new entrepreneurs and newly self-employed people over the years is that there's often the perception that if your product or service is on your website, or out on Twitter, Instagram, Facebook, LinkedIn, and other social media platforms, everybody's going to immediately come to you and purchase whatever you're offering, without any further action by you. Don't I wish it was that easy! This isn't *Field of Dreams*—even if you build it, they might not come at all. To spark action, for people to buy what you're selling, for example, you need to have processes in place, such as a sales process (which can be very simple) and a targeted marketing message to get the word out to people. You need to frame your message in a way your audience can hear you, and so on. You need to get your website out there with a strategy. You need to have clear follow-up processes in place. *And* you actually have to talk to people.

When you combine your wisdom with focused *action*—that's when the magic happens. If you have one without the other, you don't get results. And then, once you've taken action and created change, you still need to make sure that the change lasts. Change that doesn't last isn't true change.

Change Adhesive Equation: Making the Change Stick

As you proceed with change, everything that has been learned and implemented needs to "stick" and bond, just like glue, for the change to succeed. For this to happen, there has to be both support and accountability, as illustrated in the Change Adhesive Equation:

Support + Accountability = Change Adhesion

With each step you take, you'll need to consider many different variables, such as what issues people will face and what supports need to be in place to help manage or solve them. This can involve everything from training, coaching, FAQ sheets, one-on-one or group sessions, online programs, just-in-time training, guidance manuals, and more. It's about more than just developing these elements; it's also about how you use each to support the people you are engaging through the change in order to keep everything moving in the right direction. Remember, there is no one-size-fits-all solution. Every element needs to be tailored to a specific situation. Be sure to think about each possible scenario thoroughly and ensure that the necessary supports are available as you or your team need them.

Over the years, I've been fortunate to lead workshops in numerous organizations. I come in, I facilitate, I leave. While the workshop can be considered a support for the staff, what will be in place to support the application of knowledge once the workshop is over? How will the staff be able to use the new material in their day-to-day tasks or long-term projects? I can incorporate those answers during the workshop delivery, but what will happen once the participants leave the workshop?

Supports and accountability go hand in hand: without one, you can't have the other. Once the supports are set up, you can start putting accountability measures in place.

Accountability can take many forms. Specifically, with organizational change, you can help make the change stick by having managers ask their staff what they learned during the session and how they are going to use it in their day-to-day work. You can also ask staff members to send you a summary or do a presentation of what they learned at the session. Both these ideas will keep your team accountable for what they learned and how they use this new knowledge.

For accountability outside of organizational change, you may need to ask, "What are the consequences if I or

we don't do what we need to do? What happens then?"
and communicate those consequences to your staff. The
more complex the change, the more this equation needs
to be thought through.

You may also tailor accountability in terms of rewards.
For example: if I make this much money this month, I'll
buy myself a nice present! (I personally like this one.)

Making Decisions with Confidence

With the two equations above, I've endeavored to dis-
till the complexity of change into formulas you can use
to lead the change that matters to you. Change can be
intimidating, especially when you're used to doing something the same way for a long time. I've worked with
people who have talked themselves out of going for a job
interview simply because they were worried about what
they'd do if they were actually offered the job! My advice
is always to go for the interview if the job interests you.
If you're offered the job, you don't have to take it. What a
novel idea! You have a choice! It might sound simple, but
when we're under pressure and facing change, it can be
hard to think clearly and make rational, well-thought-out
decisions—as we've already seen. We can stop ourselves
in our tracks before we've done anything, which can
be good in some situations but frequently I've seen it
overused.

Change in the workplace is the same. We can sometimes get paralyzed when weighing options. When you

apply the two change equations above, you'll be able to relieve the pressure by developing an action plan made of small steps that allow you to proceed with more confidence. You can ensure your progress sticks by providing supports that are augmented with accountability measures.

As you think about how you are going to get others engaged in your ideas to take action, remember these tips to help you shape the future you want to create.

1 **Lead change instead of managing it.** Managing change is reactive and leading it is proactive—be clear about which one you are doing. There are times for both, but when you can, take ownership by demonstrating leadership through the process, regardless of your job title or how good you think you are.

2 **Talk about shifting mindsets.** Sustaining change requires a change in mindset. Encourage a shift in the mindset of the people you are working with, whether it's about meeting customer needs, how work gets done, how they work with each other, or the organization's overall model. Gather evidence, stories, data, and lessons learned to help everyone understand the mind shift that's needed.

3 **Develop the right change practices.** There are many different change models out there. I've heard a number of change practitioners and vendors say, "This is the best model," but in my experience, there are usually many options. Make the shift from employing best practices

to implementing the right practices for the particular change initiative. Recognize that these practices will need to be adjusted with each new change.

4 **Be prepared to be unprepared.** The longer and more complex the change, the less you will know what the future holds. As the person initiating this change and sharing your ideas, remember that one of the best ways to roll with the punches, so to speak, is to prepare yourself for not knowing everything. Sound simple? It's not! Sometimes, there are no answers and we just need to prepare for the unknown. It's okay to say, "I don't know."

5 **Use digital insights.** New and emerging technology is a major driver of how we get others engaged in our ideas. Technology such as artificial intelligence (AI) is becoming commonplace in our lives—for example, there's a reason you see ads on one website for things you were looking at on a completely different website. AI will lead to better data collection, the automation of repetitive tasks, and the ability to make decisions with immediate access to real-time, in-depth information. As we've learned over the last few years through the COVID-19 pandemic, being able to be agile and turn on a dime has helped us as individuals and organizations. Be aware of how data moves into and around your business, committee, or team. Take the preemptive step of mapping out how new technologies like cloud storage and AI can simplify and enhance the flow of information within your organizational

ecosystem. (Or get someone to do it for you if that's not your strength. It's not mine!)

6 **Be aware of the politics.** Competing agendas and priorities create politics during change—especially when our ideas are potentially tricky or controversial. Even if the ideas aren't that edgy, there are always competing agendas! Those of us trying to engage others in our ideas are tasked with managing our own egos, reducing uncertainty, figuring out how to satisfy the agendas that are a priority, and making sure people feel heard and acknowledged—knowing we can't solve everyone's problems and make their lives better.

TALKING POINTS

- Wisdom + Action = Change.

- Support + Accountability = Change Adhesion.

- Avoid analysis paralysis.

- Take small, simple, manageable steps.

- Be bold—and be prepared to be unprepared.

CONCLUSION
Speaking of a New World: Where We Go from Here

"It is not our abilities that show what we truly are. It is our choices."

ALBUS DUMBLEDORE, headmaster of Hogwarts

THERE'S A STORY I tell occasionally in my keynotes. It's about a man named James Dunne, an investment banker who was golfing in a town called Bedford, fifty miles north of New York City, one sunny morning. The skies were painted blue just perfectly that day; it was a gorgeous morning. His colleague and mentor, Herman Sandler, who was his partner in the investment banking firm, had told him the night before, "Take tomorrow morning off. Go enjoy the greens and golf." So, James was out on the golf course, and it was about 9:03 a.m. on the morning of September 11, 2001.

Then his caddy came up to him with a walkie-talkie, and James asked, "Oh my gosh, is something wrong with my kids?" And the caddy said, "No, a jet has just crashed into the World Trade Center." James went white. His firm's offices were on the 104th floor.

He lost 40 percent of his personnel, including his colleague and mentor Herman Sandler, that day in the World Trade Center attack. It's incredibly heartbreaking. It's still sad, decades later. In that moment, James Dunne had to juggle two things: the business and the people.

The firm lost all its computer files since we didn't have cloud service back then. But they had also lost nearly half of their staff. What could he do to make things better?

He thought about it and came up with some solutions. First and foremost, he continued salary and benefits for all the families. He created a college fund for the seventy-six children who had lost parents. By the end of the first year, he had personally attended all the funerals of the staff, including his administrative assistant. He continually focused his energy first on the remaining staff and the families of the people who had perished.

Many years later, he was asked what his biggest business insight was from that experience. James said that the more he led on the people issues, the more the business just seemed to take care of itself. People felt supported going through a horrible change and were more engaged and committed to the work.

That is a change most of us have never had to go through, though I have met many people who were directly impacted by that event over the years. But we have all gone through changes, some of them dramatic. Many of us had our lives changed overnight by the COVID-19 pandemic. When the first few cases happened, none of us could have imagined how it would disrupt our lives. But if we're here now, we have survived. Not only that, but we've also changed. Dramatically. Some of us quit our jobs and followed our true passions, realizing that life is indeed too short to waste. Others decided to devote their lives to helping others. It forced many of us to ask, "What is the change that matters to me and how can I make it happen?"

And the world keeps spinning, and there will always be change that is forced upon us: Catastrophic weather events, wars, political and financial crises. Change that we must deal with, adapt to, and raise our voices to, whether it's in support or in protest.

Keeping Your Humanity Engaged

The biggest lesson we can learn from James Dunne—and from all the other issues and inequities that happen on our planet—is that the most important thing is to keep our humanity engaged as we step forward. I believe you want to do that or you wouldn't be here reading this now.

In this book, I've shared a road map to help you spark action in yourself and others to lead and create the change that matters to you.

The starting point is having a deep understanding of what makes you tick. Get the PhD in yourself. Understand as much as you can about yourself. Beware of that nasty monster, imposter syndrome.

Next, develop your understanding of how others respond to change, especially when it's change they disagree with or that is new to them or challenges their beliefs.

We can get frustrated when people don't jump on board our ideas fast enough. Change always starts internally first with our mindset; then we can do the external processes like analyzing, planning, and implementing. Focus on mindset.

Remember that the change, the agreement, the buy-in, always starts with the other person, and it's not about you. When engaging others in your ideas, you'll think you have to have all the answers. Realizing you don't have to can free you up to have the conversations that matter to you.

When you connect the head with the heart, or the facts to the emotions, or tell the story of what the data shows, then you are more likely to spark action in others. Connect your ideas and facts to stories.

The language you use is the currency with which you engage others. The language you use can either make or break the success of whether you spark action in others. And don't ever focus on the benefits without also stating the negatives.

Take the pressure off yourself—you don't need to convince anyone of anything. Remember, a good salesperson knows they aren't there to convince you. They are there to educate and have a dialogue to spark your action.

If you're trying to spark action on tricky or hot topics, look for where you can create relatability with the other person or audience. There is always something similar. Find it!

Last but not least, use your wisdom and combine it with action. Take small, simple, manageable steps to spark action and lead change that matters to you.

You may well ask, "How can we spark action in others when there's so much noise happening all around us?" But that's exactly why we need to keep our humanity engaged. We do it in two ways: first, by ramping up our brains to pay attention to what is going on around us, and then, by leveraging the alchemy and power of language to drive our message forward.

By ramping up your brain, I don't mean feeding it Red Bull and then bingeing on social media all day long. I mean following a few good (unbiased!) news sources, which I know can be difficult to find, to keep track of what's happening in the world, and maybe one local news source as well so you can monitor your own community. Follow your industry, as well as any of your favorite topics (social justice, health, politics, technology, etc.). Have a healthy curiosity about life in general, and about the well-being of others who coinhabit this planet. These interests will serve you well when it's your turn to engage others in your ideas and consequent action toward change that matters.

Next comes something a bit more mystical. Alchemy is the magic of pulling together your ideas and forming them into the right words that connect with people in their hearts to make change happen. It is the secret potion that sneaks into the heart and makes a person *feel* rather than *think* their way toward a solution to a social problem—so they can feel a way forward instead of trying to think of a way out of it.

No matter what we disagree on, it's important to always realize that we can disagree without disrespecting each other. I think this is a fact that got lost somewhere in the comment sections of social media, or in the daily news, or maybe just because we got lazy about caring. But we need to recondition ourselves to go into each conversation, each speaking opportunity, each time when we want to engage others, with the mindset that we ourselves do not have all the answers, and that maybe we can answer many more of the questions together in a more positive way—one that brings us together instead of eviscerating us in a winner-takes-all competition.

Why do people prefer to escape the big questions and problems of life instead of working together to solve them? I think it's because fear is our default. It's easier to stay safe in our little cave of insecurity than to venture out into the open air where we can be shot down for our beliefs. But when you look at all the great periods of change in history, that is exactly the kind of courage it took for us all to move forward. And in many cases, it started with one or two strong individuals, like Gloria Steinem, Martin Luther King Jr., Florence Nightingale, Mahatma Gandhi, Nellie McClung, Nelson Mandela, Winston Churchill, and one of my favorites, a less-well-known Canadian woman, Viola Desmond—a hairdresser who in 1946, long before the modern civil rights movement, refused to move in a theater to the area that was designated for people of color at the time. She was jailed—and from there she started the fight to stop segregation, which was finally abolished in Nova Scotia in 1954.

A more recent example is Volodymyr Zelenskyy, the president of Ukraine, who was once an actor and a comedian but then stepped into a role as a world leader. When he speaks, I hear a strong, principled man, a man who when asked if he would like to leave the country to govern from abroad proudly said, "I need ammunition, not a ride." And he stayed with his troops, wearing an army uniform and looking just as haggard as they did, fighting day after day. When he managed the strength to address the United Nations, he quoted other famous leaders in history, shared graphic photos of atrocities, yet also said, "Ukraine needs peace. We need peace. Europe needs peace. The world needs peace." Watching that was heart-breaking, inspiring, moving, and action-invoking—all at the same time. At that moment, I, and likely many others watching, totally forgot he was once an actor and comedian because all I could see was a leader—and a human being—in an unimaginable and seemingly hopeless situation. It was impossible *not* to feel what he was feeling. Of course, Ukraine is not the only country on the planet experiencing deep conflicts where our empathy may lie.

Most other times, though, it's the day-to-day people like you and me who don't get named who create some of the biggest waves of change.

Why Me? Why Now?

You might think, "Who am I to raise my voice like any of these incredible people?" But amid so much chaos, now is the time for us to be positive change agents. As I mentioned above, most of us make changes that impact others, though many aren't recognized on a national and global level for that. We must find the courage within to become what my friend Beth calls "righteous troublemakers," people who create a lasting impact and meaningful change that helps others live better lives.

In order to be a "righteous troublemaker," you need to be able to take calculated risks. Not the kind where you bungee jump off a building, but where you step out of your comfort zone and acknowledge that while you may not know everything about everything, you know a few solid truths that can get an important conversation started.

Even your most personal stories can be used to make people's lives better. We come to the world to learn, to experience, to fail, and to grow. But we accomplish nothing if we keep it all inside ourselves. When we share our stories, we help ourselves and others, from our ancestors all the way to our future descendants. We keep the wisdom alive, and sometimes the memory of special people too. We work to change the outcome of the present (and possibly the future) with important information or lessons learned from the past. We take up our wands and hold the attention of another if just for a moment in time, but with the intention of sparking action and changing hearts and minds forever.

This is how we change the world. You and me. Together.

Acknowledgments

FIRST OFF, thank you to my clients and audience members. Without you, this book would not be here.

Thank you to the committed organizations, speakers bureaus, and agents that help get my work into the world.

So many people have influenced my work. I apologize in advance if I have not mentioned you here.

My deepest thanks to:

Kim Barnes for her work on influence and leadership; Linda Hoopes for her work on resilience; and Dan Pontefract for his work on talent and organizational development.

Gail Larsen for her deep wisdom and guidance on all things speaker-related.

Teal Maedel for her friendship, knowledge, and support. Lois Brummet: there are no words to describe her influence on so many levels over the last thirty years. Beth Easton for her passionate energy and deep wisdom. Steve Martindale for answering the phone. Andrew Barker for asking me to coach him all those years ago. Greg Eades for all the work and life talks. Maryse Cardin, my first paid business coaching client nearly twenty-five years ago. Amy Ruddell, one of my chief cheerleaders and feedback people. The folks I met with virtually, sometimes monthly, to chat books, speaking, and life, and who contributed in some way to this book: Hamza Khan, speaker extraordinaire; Mahfuz Chowdhury of Candybox Marketing; Phil Buckley of Change with Confidence; and B Adair, Kimberly Massi, Carolyn Crummey, Molly Parkinson, Michael Bungay Stanier, Danielle LaPorte, and others whom I text or call for quick hits of advice.

Katina Z. Jones, without whom this book would've remained an idea in my head.

The team at Page Two: Trena White, Adrineh Der-Boghossian, Cameron McKague, James Harbeck, Steph VanderMeulen, and Alison Strobel.

And last, but certainly not least, Peter Ford, who reminds me patiently to practice what I teach.

Notes

Introduction

p. 7   *describe the impact that the humiliating experience had on her:* Jennifer Knapp Wilkinson, "It May Just Be a Funny Picture to You, but That's Me in the Image," *HuffPost*, June 7, 2017, huffpost.com/entry/it-may-just-be-a-funny-picture-to-you-but-thats-me_b_5937b679e4b04ff0c46682ee.

Chapter 1: A PhD in Yourself

p. 15   *You need to share your "original medicine":* for more on the concept of original medicine, see Gail Larsen, *Transformational Speaking: If You Want to Change the World, Tell a Better Story* (Berkeley: Celestial Arts, 2009).

p. 20   *a 2020 study on imposter syndrome:* Dena M. Bravata et al., "Prevalence, Predictors, and Treatment of Impostor Syndrome: A Systematic Review," *Journal of General Internal Medicine* 35, no. 4 (April 2020): 1252–75, doi.org//10.1007/s11606-019-05364-1.

p. 23   *Research shows we tend to overestimate risk:* Kristina M. Hengen and Georg W. Alpers, "What's the Risk? Fearful Individuals Generally Overestimate Negative Outcomes and They Dread Outcomes of Specific Events," *Frontiers in Psychology* 10 (2019), doi.org/10.3389/fpsyg.2019.01676; Meg Jay, "What to Do When Your Mind (Always) Dwells on the Worst-Case Scenario," *Harvard Business Review*, September 15, 2020, hbr.org/2020/09/what-to-do-when-your-mind-always-dwells-on-the-worst-case-scenario.

p. 23   *"There's nothing enlightened about shrinking:* Marianne
         Williamson, *A Return to Love: Reflections on the Principles of
         "A Course in Miracles"* (New York: Harper Perennial, 1996),
         191.

Chapter 2: Your Brain

p. 27   *for more about this, read:* Amy Arnsten, Carolyn M.
         Mazure, and Rajita Sinha, "This Is Your Brain in
         Meltdown," *Scientific American* 306, no. 4 (April 2012):
         48–53, doi.org//10.1038/scientificamerican0412-48.

p. 29   *the "amygdala hijack":* Daniel Goleman, *Emotional
         Intelligence: Why It Can Matter More Than IQ* (New York:
         Bantam, 2005).

p. 31   *the RAS is a collection of neurons:* For a simple explanation
         of the RAS, see "RAS (Reticular Activating System),"
         University of Minnesota Extension, Two for You
         video, episode 1.5, 2:18, extension.umn.edu/
         two-you-video-series/ras.

p. 31   *You could describe it as your attention filter:* Daniel J. Levitin,
         *The Organized Mind: Thinking Straight in the Age of
         Information Overload* (New York: Dutton, 2014).

p. 34   *We respond very differently to change that's disruptive:* Linda
         Hoopes and Mark Kelly, *Managing Change with Personal
         Resilience: 21 Keys for Bouncing Back & Staying on Top in
         Turbulent Organizations* (Mark Kelly Books, 2003).

Chapter 3: Be an Apprentice to Change

p. 43   *we need to set goals we can see ourselves reaching:*
         Madhuleena Roy Chowdhury, "The Science & Psychology
         of Goal-Setting 101," PositivePsychology.com, May 2, 2019,
         positivepsychology.com/goal-setting-psychology/.

p. 44   *"listening seems to make an employee more relaxed:*
         Guy Itzchakov and Avi Kluger, "The Power of Listening
         in Helping People Change," *Harvard Business Review*,
         May 17, 2018, hbr.org/2018/05/the-power-of-listening-in-
         helping-people-change.

Chapter 4: Lead at the Edge of Change

p. 53 *gratitude works for me and the research backs this up:*
Joshua Brown and Joel Wong, "How Gratitude
Changes You and Your Brain," *Greater Good Magazine*,
June 6, 2017, greatergood.berkeley.edu/article/item/
how_gratitude_changes_you_and_your_brain.

p. 53 *This phenomenon is known as the self-fulfilling prophecy:*
Courtney E. Ackerman, "Self-Fulfilling Prophecy in
Psychology," PositivePsychology.com, May 1, 2018,
positivepsychology.com/self-fulfilling-prophecy.

Chapter 5: Cocreate Change

p. 68 *"That which we witness:* For more on Angeles Arrien's
work, see thefourdirections.com/angeles.

Chapter 6: Shape the Future

p. 71 *Indiana had to cross a huge chasm: Indiana Jones and
the Last Crusade*, directed by Steven Spielberg (Hollywood,
CA: Paramount Pictures, 1989).

p. 74 *a study on dishwashing:* Virginia Satir, *The New
Peoplemaking* (Palo Alto, CA: Science and Behavior Books,
1988), 224-25.

Chapter 7: Design the Story You Will Tell

p. 93 *comedian Gilda Radner said:* Gilda Radner, *It's Always
Something*, 20th anniversary/revised ed. (New York:
Simon & Schuster, 2009), 254.

Chapter 9: Go Deeper

p. 118 *the outcome changes because there is empathy:* For more
on empathy and vulnerability, check out Brené Brown's
book *Daring Greatly: How the Courage to Be Vulnerable
Transforms the Way We Live, Love, Parent, and Lead*
(New York: Avery, 2012).

Chapter 11: Get Past "No"

p. 146 *the number one job of leaders:* Sunnie Giles,
"The Most Important Leadership Competencies,
According to Leaders Around the World," *Harvard
Business Review*, March 15, 2016, hbr.org/2016/03/
the-most-important-leadership-competencies-
according-to-leaders-around-the-world.

Conclusion

p. 166 *his biggest business insight was from that experience:* Eric J.
McNulty and Leonard Marcus, "Are You Leading Through
the Crisis... or Managing the Response?" *Harvard Business
Review*, March 25, 2020, hbr.org/2020/03/are-you-leading-
through-the-crisis-or-managing-the-response.

p. 170 *when asked if he would like to leave the country:* Sharon
Braithwaite, "Zelensky Refuses US Offer to Evacuate,
Saying 'I Need Ammunition, Not a Ride,'" CNN, February
26, 2022, cnn.com/2022/02/26/europe/ukraine-zelensky-
evacuation-intl/index.html.

p. 170 *managed the strength to address the United Nations:*
Volodymyr Zelenskyy, "Speech by the President of Ukraine
at a Meeting of the UN Security Council," Presidential
Office of Ukraine, April 5, 2022, president.gov.ua/en/news/
vistup-prezidenta-ukrayini-na-zasidanni-radi-bezpeki-
oon-74121.

Further Reading

HERE ARE SOME books and authors that I've found helpful and may interest you:

Adam Grant's books
Change on the Run, by Phil Buckley
Changing for Good, by James O. Prochaska, John C. Norcross, and Carlo C. DiClemente
Creating Healthy Organizations, by Graham Lowe
Emotional Intelligence, by Daniel Goleman
Exercising Influence, by B. Kim Barnes
The Fire Starter Sessions, by Danielle LaPorte
The Four-Fold Way, by Angeles Arrien
GuRu, by RuPaul
Mindset, by Carol Dweck
The Only Certain Freedom, by Patrick O'Neill
Prosilience, by Linda Hoopes
The Purpose Effect, by Dan Pontefract
Self-Efficacy, by Albert Bandura
Transformational Speaking, by Gail Larsen
What Got You Here Won't Get You There, by Marshall Goldsmith
Your Brain at Work, by David Rock

About the Author

GREGG BROWN'S CAREER working with people began when he was ten years old: he sat his friends down at a chalkboard to teach them math. *Not* one of his strongest subjects. Throughout his teens, he taught canoeing and crafts at summer camp. He did much better there.

Surviving all that, over thirty years ago, Gregg was part of the groundbreaking team that opened the first wave of Starbucks stores in Canada.

To further sharpen his skills and understand how people tick, Gregg worked with prisoners in maximum-security federal penitentiaries and pioneered numerous social change programs in the community.

Jumping into the organizational world and improving how we work together and how we think has been at the core of Gregg's work since then, as work is where we spend most of our time!

Now, as an in-demand global speaker and advisor, Gregg engages people all over the world to help them build the courage to wade into the never-ending waves of change. His audiences include Fortune 500 companies, governments, not-for-profits, and international humanitarian organizations, among others.

Gregg volunteers with and mentors entrepreneurs of all ages and experience including veterans, ex-military, and youth, as he believes small businesses and entrepreneurs build community and create opportunities for people to express their creativity in the world.

His ideas on change, leadership, and the future of work are published in media such as *Forbes, Newsweek, Rolling Stone*, and *Entrepreneur*.

Gregg holds a master's in social science from the University of Leicester in the UK, with a focus on organizational psychology, leadership, and performance, and is an associate member of the American Psychological Association.

Want to spark action and lead change that matters in your organization, or just simply change the world one small step at a time?

Reach out to me!

I'm always happy to have
a chat to see if I can help:
info@greggbrown.ca

For ideas and articles:
linkedin.com/in/greggbrown1

Stay in touch here for insights and
random fun pics on Instagram:
@greggbrownTO

For additional resources, articles,
and videos, check out my website:
bechangeready.com

#ChangeTheWorld: You can do it!